ISRAEL, THE PALESTINIANS, AND THE ADMINISTRATION'S PEACE PLAN

HEARING

BEFORE THE

SUBCOMMITTEE ON THE MIDDLE EAST AND NORTH AFRICA

OF THE

COMMITTEE ON FOREIGN AFFAIRS
HOUSE OF REPRESENTATIVES

ONE HUNDRED FIFTEENTH CONGRESS

SECOND SESSION

FEBRUARY 14, 2018

Serial No. 115–112

Printed for the use of the Committee on Foreign Affairs

Available via the World Wide Web: http://www.foreignaffairs.house.gov/ or
http://www.gpo.gov/fdsys/

U.S. GOVERNMENT PUBLISHING OFFICE

28–655PDF   WASHINGTON : 2018

For sale by the Superintendent of Documents, U.S. Government Publishing Office
Internet: bookstore.gpo.gov   Phone: toll free (866) 512–1800; DC area (202) 512–1800
Fax: (202) 512–2104   Mail: Stop IDCC, Washington, DC 20402–0001

C O N T E N T S

Page

WITNESSES

LETTERS, STATEMENTS, ETC., SUBMITTED FOR THE HEARING

APPENDIX

ISRAEL, THE PALESTINIANS, AND THE ADMINISTRATION'S PEACE PLAN

House of Representatives,
Subcommittee on the Middle East and North Africa,
Committee on Foreign Affairs,
Washington, DC.

The subcommittee met, pursuant to notice, at 2:24 p.m., in room 2172, Rayburn House Office Building, Hon. Ileana Ros-Lehtinen (chairman of the subcommittee) presiding.

Ms. Ros-Lehtinen. The members of the subcommittee will come to order.

Boy, I really hustled from our Lady Members American Heart Health photo. And I get over here, and Ann Wagner is already here, you know, with her fourth Cuban cafecito, and I hustled. I have got to get in shape.

After recognizing myself and Ranking Member Deutch for our opening statements, I will then recognize other members seeking recognition for 1 minute.

We will then hear from our witnesses. I apologize, 20 minutes late and more. And without objection, the witnesses' prepared statements will be made a part of the record, and members may have 5 days to insert statements and questions for the record, subject to the length limitation in the rules. The chair now recognizes herself.

During the campaign and since he took office, President Trump has repeatedly stated that it is his mission to achieve the ultimate deal. A negotiated peaceful settlement between Israelis and Palestinians, a simple task, as anyone who has ever heard of the Israeli-Palestinian conflict can tell you. Administration after administration, Secretary of State, after Secretary of State, all have had their eyes on the prize. Broker a peace deal between the Israelis and Palestinians and your name will be etched in the history books for all time.

At this point in any previous administration, we would convene and ask ourselves the very same questions we always ask. Does the administration have a legitimate chance of brokering peace? What will it take to bring the parties to together to the negotiation table? What will the peace process look like? And can we build enough support and momentum to move the process forward?

I am sure we would inevitably hear many of the same things: The status quo has not changed, the negotiation partners remain the same. But we remain hopeful, always hopeful, despite the fact that the players remain the same and we keep trying the same approach. Only this time, for better or for worse, we don't have the answers.

We can't say for certain how we expect things to go because this administration has fundamentally changed the status quo. First, the administration allowed the waiver on the PLO office to lapse in November, limiting Palestinian activity in their DC office to strictly peace-process-related activity.

This was the first time an administration had done this. Then in December, the administration announced that the U.S. officially recognized Jerusalem as the capital of Israel, and that we would be moving our Embassy to the capital. This was the right decision. It wasn't just morally right, but it was also implementing long-standing U.S. law, which mandated that U.S. recognized Jerusalem as Israel's capital.

Then the administration withheld U.S. contributions to UNRWA, a decision I support, and I hope we go further until we see much-needed reforms at this agency.

These are the steps that no previous administration has taken, yet I believe they are long overdue, and I believe they are rooted in solid policy, ultimately aimed at wielding the leverage we have to further our own interests, but also to achieve peace between Israelis and Palestinians.

Every administration that has come before has always operated in the same space, strictly diplomacy. This is an agreement between two parties, one a sovereign state, and the other, a people aiming to realize their own statehood. So the only way to resolve this, according to the conventional wisdom, is through diplomacy.

But the Trump administration has approached this like a business deal. Not only has this upset the status quo, but it has thrown the Palestinian leadership into a "what?" kind of mode. They knew how to respond to every approach we made. Now, they are in unchartered territory. And this may work to our advantage, and ultimately, to the advantage of peace for the region.

Some observers have stated that the administration has no real peace plan, and that it is making it up as it goes along. I am not so sure, and I think that we can see a pattern with the administration's decisions in recent months.

It is unlikely that the President would make such clear statements about his desire to achieve the ultimate deal if he had no real intent to do so. After all, this is a man who prides himself on his deal-making skills. But critics are right to be concerned. The administration should have done more groundwork, presented a plan before making unilateral decisions. It would have given us a better chance to not only build our own case, but to build support from other actors, particularly the Arab states.

It is hard to imagine getting an agreement without our being able to get support from these Arab states. And it should make clear to us, and to the parties, what its blueprint for peace is, because right now, all parties are uncertain what to expect from the administration, and at any given moment, the administration may change its objectives. We have seen that before.

What we need now is a clear and decisive statement of intent from the administration. I hope that our panel can elaborate on

what the administration can do to advance the prospects of peace,
a peace we all have long pursued.

Thank you again. And now I am so proud to yield to my friend
and ranking member, Mr. Deutch of Florida.

Mr. DEUTCH. Thank you, Madam Chairman. I appreciate the opportunity to examine an issue that you and I have worked very
closely on for many years. Support for Israel and peace and security in the Middle East has always enjoyed deep bipartisan support
in Congress. And it is my hope that today we continue to affirm
that support.

I want to thank our witnesses for appearing. I want to especially
thank Ambassador Shapiro for coming in from Israel to offer his
unparalleled insight into these issues after 6 years as our American Ambassador to Israel.

Madam Chairman, I must say that I am struck by the title of
today's hearing because we don't, in fact, know what the administration's peace plan is. And to the extent we are aware, no such
plan exists. We have seen the President's envoy for international
negotiation spend considerable time in the region getting to know
the parties. That is positive. We have seen the President's son-in-law travel the Gulf, apparently trying to persuade our Arab allies
to buy into some kind of push for peace. All of this is well and good.
And this is certainly not the first administration to struggle with
how to proceed here.

What concerns me, and what I hope we have the opportunity to
discuss today, is how approaching this issue without a strategy is
potentially damaging to the prospects for peace and, ultimately, to
U.S. interests.

In February 2017, Israeli Prime Minister Netanyahu visited the
White House. During public remarks, President Trump indicated
that he would support whatever solution the parties agreed upon,
saying, I am looking at two states and one state, and then he said
he can live with either one.

This marked a serious departure from longstanding U.S. policy
backed by multiple international resolutions, but the only path to
lasting peace is two states for two peoples, a safe and secure Israel
living side-by-side with a prosperous Palestinian state, achieved
through direct negotiations between the two parties.

And that is challenging now, but this distancing has rightfully
alarmed many, myself included, who believe that without American
leadership working toward a two-state solution, our own security
interests may be at risk as well.

Israel is our strongest ally in the region. The security cooperation
between our two countries is a vital component of our national security and of Israel's security. And there must be no question that
the U.S. is committed to Israel security, as evidenced by the signing of an unprecedented new 10-year, $38 billion MOU negotiated
by the Obama administration.

It is really unsettling that when asked in an interview this week
if Israel has the right to defend itself if Iran establishes permanent
basis in Syria and Lebanon, the President said, "I don't want to
comment on that right now."

I fear that the current administration is playing fast and loose
with diplomacy. In December, the President recognized Jerusalem

as Israel's capital. And I want to join you, Madam Chairman, in stating unequivocally, that Jerusalem is and always will be the capital of Israel. But the decision to recognize Jerusalem didn't seem to be accompanied by any broader plan from the administration.

In an interview this week, President Trump said that he has taken Jerusalem off the table. He also said that both sides would have to make hard compromises. Again, this just begs the question, what is the administration's plan and what is it ultimately hoping to achieve?

The administration has worked hard to cultivate support from the Gulf. And the idea that those countries will play a role in pushing the Palestinians to negotiations, and, in turn, a deal, would see a new normalization of relations between Israel and the Arab states. That is not new. But the administration seemed to give a good faith effort to getting the Saudis and others on board.

Then on Monday, the President tweeted that the U.S. has so stupidly spent $7 trillion in the Middle East. Well, we have spent money in the Middle East. We have spent it, obviously, in Israel; we have spent it in Jordan and Egypt to protect our mutual security interests, including Israel's security; we spent it to bolster our allies and our joint fight against ISIS and to counter Iranian threats. None of this spending is "stupid."

Further, even as his envoys talk up Palestinian economic development, the President seems to be ignoring a potential humanitarian crisis in Gaza that most in Israel have expressed deep concern about, and instead, has haphazardly cut off humanitarian assistance.

Now, no one can argue that the best thing to ensure Israel's security is peace, but that is exceedingly more difficult when President Abbas, in his 14th year of a 4-year term, continues to desperately try to avoid direct negotiations, going to every capital looking for support and suggesting that he may leave Oslo.

Now, I am not naive to the challenges at this moment facing the two-state solution. When we have conflicting and confusing messages coming from the U.S. Ambassador to Israel, the President's special envoy and the President himself, it makes it easier for members of Israel's Parliament to push a bill calling for the annexation of the West Bank, or for a prominent minister to say that Israel should ignore the U.S. on the issue of annexation.

These are really difficult issues. Calls to cut off all humanitarian assistance and security assistance to the Palestinians has a very real impact on the lives of Palestinians, on their security, and on Israel's security.

That said, we cannot look the other way when the PA continues to pay terrorists who carry out attacks against Israeli citizens. That is why the House passed the Taylor Force Act, and we urged the Senate to do the same.

Madam Chairman, this committee has typically taken a bipartisan approach on foreign aid, on assistance that promotes human rights, on economic development, and security. We had bipartisan support for the Taylor Force Act and for Iran sanctions. Bipartisan support for Israel as it faces new threats along its northern border from Iranian presence in Syria and Lebanon, and we have historically had bipartisan support for a two-state solution for two peoples living side-by-side in peace and security.

I just ask that as we hear from our very well-informed and insightful witnesses, that we keep this spirit of bipartisanship in mind as we go forward here, and in particular, as we address these issues in Congress.

Thank you, Madam Chairman.

Ms. ROS-LEHTINEN. Very good. Thank you so much, Mr. Deutch. And that would be my intention as well. Thank you, my good friend.

And now we will hear from our members. And I apologize again for being so late. And we will start with, keeping the Florida delegation groove going, Mr. DeSantis of Florida.

Mr. DESANTIS. Thank you, Madam Chairman.

The President's decision to recognize Jerusalem was long overdue. It was the right decision. People had said, oh, you have to have a final settlement. But we have been doing this for 25 years. It has been the same outcomes over and over again. This shakes it up. It sends a direct signal to Palestinian Arabs: You are not going to drive Israel into the sea. You need to recognize their right to exist as a Jewish state, which you have never been willing to do. You need to stop funding the families of terrorists who murder Israelis. And then we will see if there is progress to be made.

But I think the President's posture is right. He is basically saying he is going to support our strong ally Israel. He is not going to, hopefully, shoehorn them into making decisions that are going to be detrimental to their security. And I think that is the posture that we have to take.

I am glad that we are having this hearing. I want to hear what the witnesses have to say. But at the end of the day, history has shown the Israelis have been willing to make really strong sacrifices, make really strong concessions—heck, concessions I probably wouldn't have been willing to make. But the Palestinian Arabs have never been willing to accept the legitimacy of a Jewish state in the Middle East.

I yield back.

Ms. ROS-LEHTINEN. Thank you so much, Ron.

Mr. Cicilline of Rhode Island.

Mr. CICILLINE. Thank you, Chairman Ros-Lehtinen and Ranking Member Deutch, for holding this hearing today.

And thank you to our witnesses for being here.

I have to say, like Ranking Member Deutch, I was really surprised when I saw the title of this hearing, "Israel, the Palestinians, and the Administration's Peace Plan." I was surprised and excited to hear that the administration has a peace plan for the Israeli-Palestinian conflict. I can't wait to see it. But I am left wondering if it is one of those secret plans the President seems to be so fond of or one that we will ever get to see.

And while I am thrilled to be welcoming such a distinguished and knowledgeable panel to testify before us today, I have to wonder, if we are going to have a hearing about the administration's peace plan for the Israeli-Palestinian conflict, would it not make sense to have someone from the administration here to testify about it?

But then I have to wonder, who would we have testify? Who exactly within the administrationis driving the policy on the Israeli-Palestinian issue? Is it Jared Kushner? Ambassador Friedman? Vice President Pence? Secretary Tillerson? The President himself? And, in the meantime, the position of Assistant Secretary for the Near Eastern Affairs Bureau remains unfilled.

As much as I appreciate the hearing today, I think it highlights the fact that this administration has so far articulated no coherent policy for dealing with the Israeli-Palestinian conflict. In fact, the competing voices, incoherent policy decisions, and lack of senior-level appointees only serves to further muddle this already complex issue.

I hope our witnesses can shed some light on what is happening within the administration and whether a reasonable observer can discern any coherent policy out of the statements made and the steps that the administration has taken thus far. And I remain ever hopeful of that.

And, with that, I yield back.

Ms. ROS-LEHTINEN. Thank you so much, David.

Mr. Donovan of New York.

Mr. DONOVAN. Thank you, Madam Chairwoman.

A path to peace between Israel and the Palestinian people is a complex process but one that is necessary to bring stability in the Middle East. I want to see all people thrive, but Hamas and the Palestinian Authority both make this impossible, with their infighting and a policy of paying out terrorists and terrorist families.

Terrorism breeds violence and resentment, and the United States must do everything in its power to end it. The only simple part of this difficult issue is reconciliation cannot start until terrorism supported by Hamas, the Palestinian Authority, and other groups ends.

I thank you, Madam Chairwoman, and I yield the remainder of my time.

Ms. ROS-LEHTINEN. Thank you so much, Mr. Donovan.

And Mr. Schneider of Illinois.

Mr. SCHNEIDER. Thank you, Madam Chairman. Thank you both to you and to the ranking member for having this hearing; to our witnesses for being here today.

As has already been said, I have spent my entire life praying for, working for, peace for Israel and her neighbors, a peace that would be two states, living in prosperity, with security. A Jewish state of Israel, with Jerusalem as its capital, as it has been for the Jewish people for 3,000 years.

It is critical that the U.S. has a role in this. Over the course of my lifetime, I remember in the 1970s first when Sadat went to Jerusalem and the role the United States had in achieving peace between Israel and Egypt; in the 1990s, as the dynamic was changing, the role the United States played in ensuring and delivering peace between Israel and Jordan.

And so, if there is to be peace, it must come with a U.S. role—a U.S. role that recognizes Israel is our strongest, most important ally in the region, recognizes that Israel must have security as a Jewish state, but recognizes that without the United States, Israel can't have the confidence to proceed.

I look forward to the testimony today. And, with that, I yield back.

Ms. ROS-LEHTINEN. Thank you so much, Brad.

Mr. Mast of Florida.

Mr. MAST. Thank you, madam.

You know, peace has been elusive, but it is my opinion that it is closer and more attainable than it has ever actually been, and that is because of the blunt honesty that is finally being applied to our foreign policy.

You look at what has gone on year after year. The Palestinian Authority, much of the Middle East, much of the world, they pretend, because of the sensitivities of a few, that Jerusalem is not Israel's capital. America has said, "We will no longer pretend."

And you look, year after year, the Palestinian Authority's chief negotiating tool is terror—bombings, stabbings, shootings, driving over people, rocket attacks. They do that with one hand, while with the other hand they shop around the United Nations for anybody that will naively view them as a victim, all while receiving U.S. aid, only to turn it over as blood money to the terrorists and the families who attack Israel. Congress and the President have said, "No more blood money."

I believe that peace is more possible than ever because, finally, our foreign policy is reflecting that we are not going to pursue peace and negotiate peace with our enemies. We are only going to pursue peace with those who can declare and demonstrate that they are a former enemy, and that is the place that we need to be.

Ms. ROS-LEHTINEN. Thank you, Brian.

Mr. Suozzi of New York.

Mr. SUOZZI. Thank you, Madam Chairwoman.

Thank you to our distinguished witnesses for being here today. Missing from the table, however, are the administration officials. I do hope that one day Congress can get a clear picture of the administration's plan from our colleagues over at the executive branch. Palestinians have spent the past 2 months complaining about the President's decision to recognize Jerusalem as Israel's capital. I supported that decision then, and I still support it now. It was the long overdue recognition of a reality. Jerusalem has been the seat of Israel's Government for decades and the focal point of Jewish life for millennia. And, in many ways, it was a symbolic decision. It hasn't changed the realities on the ground, and any effort to blame that decision for ending a peace process that was defunct to begin with is disingenuous.

But exactly that is the plan of the Palestinians. For almost a year, the Palestinians met with the President's team over 20 times. Mr. Abbas himself met with President Trump personally on four occasions. And now, before we have even heard what the administration's peace plan is, the Palestinians have pulled out of the process.

Recently, Mr. Abbas was in Sochi meeting with Vladimir Putin. He wants the Russians to take over the negotiations, the same Russians who have backed a murderous regime in neighboring Syria. A regime that just this weekend, allowed Iran to menace Israel with a military drone and then shot down an Israel jet.

Sadly, this is the same double game that is not new, and it has always been played. For too long, they say they want to resume negotiations with Israel even as they pursue unilateral diplomatic moves against Israel. They say they oppose violence even as the Palestinian Authority pays millions of dollars to families of terrorists, a demented practice that this Congress is trying to end.

We all want to see an end to this endless conflict. We need to know the administration's plan, and we need the Palestinians to stop playing games.

Ms. ROS-LEHTINEN. Thank you, Tom.

Mr. Rohrabacher of California.

Mr. ROHRABACHER. Thank you very much.

I am very happy to discuss the new policies, even though they are yet to be defined, because at least we know that we are going to replace the policies of the last administration that created havoc in the Middle East, undermined all the moderate forces in the Middle East, and unleashed radical Islamic terrorists throughout the region. Yeah, whatever we do to discard those policies, that is a good policy, in my mind.

You know, we have Israel always under attack in situations like this. They are always under attack because supposedly they are to blame for not giving up more to the Palestinians. And let's just note: Israel over the last three decades has given up the West Bank, they have given up authority there, all of Gaza. They have withdrawn totally from the Sinai Desert. All they want is not to be attacked, and they can't even get that agreement enforced.

Right now we understand the Palestinians have given up nothing. If there is a roadblock to peace, let's focus on trying to pressure the Palestinians instead of trying to pressure Israel, and let's reward Israel, the way our President has just done.

Thank you very much.

Ms. ROS-LEHTINEN. Thank you, Dana.

Mr. Lieu of California.

Mr. LIEU. Thank you, Madam Chair. Thank you for calling this hearing.

I do want to echo what some of my colleagues have said, which is that it is not helpful to have zero administration officials here talking about the administration's peace plan.

Jared Kushner in December said that we know the details in the plan. I actually don't believe him. I don't believe there is a plan. But we should have him here to testify under oath about what the plan is. It is also important to note: Does he run Middle East policy, or is it the Secretary of State, or is it somebody else?

So we don't have administration officials here to talk about what is in a plan and we don't even know who is running Middle East policy. It is not helpful, I think, very much for this hearing to just sort of guess at what is actually happening in the White House.

I do appreciate the witnesses being here. I do look forward to hearing what you are going to guess about. But, ultimately, we are going to have to have administration officials here.

I yield back.

Ms. ROS-LEHTINEN. Thank you so much, Ted.

Ms. Frankel of Florida.

Ms. FRANKEL. Thank you, Madam Chair. I will be very quick, which is this—and I appreciate everything all my colleagues have said.

This is such a contentious Congress, we fight about everything. I think it is very important that there is one thing we do not fight about, the peace and security of Israel. And I hope it maintains itself as a bipartisan issue.

And I yield back.

Ms. ROS-LEHTINEN. Thank you very much.

And seeing no—Mr. Zeldin of New York. I apologize.

Mr. ZELDIN. Well, thank you, Madam Chair.

Just to share some thoughts, after hearing some of my colleagues speaking about, with curiosity, as to the administration's chain of command inside of the White House. My understanding is that Jared Kushner, Jason Greenblatt, and H.R. McMaster, the Secretary of State—in charge of the State Department policy—Ambassador Haley as the Ambassador to the United Nations—doing whatever is in her lane as the United States Ambassador to the United Nations—are all under a chain of command reporting to the President of the United States. Make the decisions as it relates to moving the Embassy from Tel Aviv to Jerusalem, recognizing Jerusalem as the capital of Israel, choosing to better leverage our aid that we provide to the United Nations, and cutting off aid to the Palestinians as long as they continue to incite violence and financially reward terrorism.

So that is the chain of command that reports to the President of the United States. Those are the people running it inside the White House, in the State Department, and at the United Nations. It is pretty clear to me and to others who have been paying attention.

I yield back.

Ms. ROS-LEHTINEN. Thank you so much, Lee.

And now it is my honor to introduce our panelists.

Thank you again for your patience.

First, we are delighted to welcome back Mr. Clifford May, founder and president of the Foundation for Defense of Democracies. Prior to this post, Mr. May was a foreign correspondent and editor for The New York Times and other publications. And in 2016, Mr. May was appointed to the United States Commission on International Religious Freedom by Senator Mitch McConnell.

Thank you for being here today, Clifford, and we look forward to your testimony, sir.

Then, we will be delighted to welcome Mr. Ghaith al-Omari—did I do okay? Thank you, Ghaith. Ghaith is the senior fellow of the Irwin Levy Family Program on the U.S.-Israel Strategic Relationship at the Washington Institute for Near East Policy. Prior to this position, he served in various roles within the Palestinian Authority, including as adviser to the negotiation team during the 1999 to 2001 permanent status talks.

We are very excited for your testimony. Thank you so much for joining us.

And, finally, we are so delighted to welcome to our subcommittee a good friend of most of us here in the subcommittee, Ambassador Daniel Shapiro. He is currently the visiting fellow at Tel Aviv University's Institute of National Security Studies. And prior to this position, of course, Ambassador Shapiro served as our Ambassador to Israel during the previous administration. Among his many other positions, Ambassador Shapiro has also served as Senior Director for the Middle East and North Africa on the National Security Council.

Thank you. It is great to see you again. And you always made time to visit with all of the delegations that came over to Israel. It is so great to have you here.

So we will begin with you, Mr. May, and then work down the line. Thank you, Cliff.

STATEMENT OF MR. CLIFFORD D. MAY, FOUNDER AND PRESIDENT, FOUNDATION FOR DEFENSE OF DEMOCRACIES

Mr. MAY. Madam Chairman, Ranking Member Deutch, members of the subcommittee, on behalf of the Foundation for Defense of Democracies, I thank you for this opportunity to testify.

As you pointed out just now, there have been significant changes in U.S. relations with Israel and the Palestinian Authority—among them, U.S. recognition of Jerusalem as the capital of the Jewish state, the withholding of some assistance from UNRWA until it provides greater transparency, and an attempt to counter actions at the U.N. intended to demonize and delegitimize Israel.

All this is taking place as the Trump administration attempts to build their new regional framework with the Arab Sunni states, threatened by the hegemonic ambitions of the Islamic Republic of Iran. These states now recognize that their security interests with Israel coincide.

Despite these developments, all deserving of your support, I am going to argue that any new peace process should be seen as only preliminary—small steps, but in the right direction. It is unlikely that the Palestinian-Israeli conflict can be resolved in the foreseeable future.

One of the reasons why became vivid last weekend when Iran provoked a clash with Israel. Note that no Palestinian leader condemned this Iranian provocation, no Palestinian leader has ever condemned the Iranian regime, whose intentions toward Israel are openly exterminationist.

Hezbollah, Tehran's proxy, has tens of thousands of missiles pointing at Israeli targets from Lebanon, a country that it now effectively rules. Hezbollah is openly genocidal toward both Israelis and Jews. Hezbollah's leader, Hassan Nasrallah, has said, "If the Jews will gather from all parts of the world into occupied Palestine, there the final and decisive battle will take place." Hamas, the major power in Gaza, holds identical views about Israelis and Jews.

In this environment, it would require a Palestinian leader of enormous independence, charisma, and courage to negotiate a resolution of the conflict with Israel. Mahmoud Abbas is not that leader.

Elected to a 4-year term as Palestinian Authority President in 2005, Mr. Abbas has remained in that position without benefit of reelection. In recent statements, he made it clear that he does not accept the basic premise of a two-state solution, two states for two peoples, one of those peoples being the Jewish people. He does not recognize that the Jewish people have a right to self-determination in any part of their ancient homeland. He recently said that Jerusalem is Arab, Muslim, and Christian, conspicuously omitting Jerusalem's Jewish roots.

It has been years since Mr. Abbas has been willing to negotiate with Israelis. Instead, he has taken part in a campaign to delegitimize Israel. This includes U.N. Security Council Resolution 2334, which asserts that Israel has no rights in eastern Jerusalem—not even the Jewish quarter of the old city; not even Judaism's holiest sites, the Western Wall and the Temple Mount.

The administration's recognition of Jerusalem as Israel's capital has at least helped halt the momentum of this very destructive narrative. It is important to understand, this campaign has the strategic intent of justifying attacks against Israel by Iran, Hezbollah, Hamas, and others as a resistance to an illegitimate regime that sooner or later is to be fatally poisoned by a cocktail of violence, economic warfare, and diplomacy.

At some point after Mr. Abbas leaves the scene, a new peace process may be developed, but that will depend on who succeeds him. According to Palestinian basic law, after 60 days there are to be free elections. How likely is that? And if, as has been the pattern in the Middle East for centuries, power is taken by force of arms instead, who is likely to prevail? Hamas? Hezbollah? Other jihadi groups?

Working with Saudi Arabia and other partners, perhaps it may be possible to develop a next generation of Palestinian leaders who do not view peaceful coexistence with Israel as tantamount to defeat, but the magnitude of this challenge cannot be overstated.

I elaborate on these and other issues in my written testimony and offer more than a dozen recommendations—small steps in the right direction. I look forward to your questions. Thank you.

[The prepared statement of Mr. May follows:]

House Foreign Affairs Committee, Subcommittee on Middle East and North Africa

Israel, the Palestinians, and the Administration's Peace Plan

CLIFFORD D. MAY

Founder and President
Foundation for Defense of Democracies

Washington, DC
February 14, 2018

FDD
FOUNDATION FOR
DEFENSE OF DEMOCRACIES

www.defenddemocracy.org

Clifford D. May   February 14, 2018

Chairman Ros-Lehtinen, Ranking Member Deutch, members of the subcommittee, on behalf of the Foundation for Defense of Democracies, thank you for the opportunity to testify.

Over the past year, there have been significant changes in U.S. relations with both Israel and the Palestinian Authority (PA). Among them: U.S. recognition of Jerusalem as the capital of the Jewish state, threats to withhold assistance from the Palestinian Authority unless it undertakes reforms, and the withholding of some assistance to the United Nations Relief and Works Agency (UNRWA) unless it provides greater transparency. In addition, there has been an attempt to counter actions taken at the United Nations to delegitimize and demonize Israel.

All this is taking place as the Trump administration endeavors to build a new regional "framework" with the Arab/Sunni states who are threatened by the hegemonic – one might say imperialist – ambitions of the Islamic Republic of Iran, which is majority Persian and Shiite. These states are less hostile to Israel – the enemy of their enemy – than ever before.

President Trump has hoped to utilize this changed architecture to revive the Palestinian-Israeli peace process and make the "ultimate deal." Despite these steps and developments – all positive and deserving of your support and encouragement – I am going to argue that any new peace process should be seen as only preliminary. It is unlikely that the Palestinian-Israeli conflict can be resolved in the foreseeable future.

That was true a week ago for reasons I will endeavor to explain. But initiating a new and improved peace process has become even more problematic following what transpired over the weekend. Iranian forces, operating from an airbase in Syria, sent a drone into Israeli airspace. An Israeli Apache helicopter downed it. Israel then sent eight F-16s to destroy the Iranian command center in Syria. One of the jets was overwhelmed by what the Israelis describe as "massive Syrian anti-air fire." The pilot of that plane returned to Israeli airspace where he and his navigator ejected. Both survived. Their plane crashed on Israeli territory.[1] The region is on high alert; more conflict may lie ahead.

You will note that no Palestinian leader condemned this Iranian provocation. No Palestinian leader has ever condemned the Iranian regime, whose intentions toward Israel are openly annihilationist.

Hezbollah, Tehran's proxy militia, has tens of thousands of missiles pointing at Israeli targets from Lebanon, a country it now effectively rules. Hezbollah is openly genocidal toward both Israelis and Jews. The leader of the "Party of God," Hassan Nasrallah, has said: if "the Jews will gather from all parts of the world into occupied Palestine ... there the final and decisive battle will take place."[2]

Hamas, the major power in Gaza, and a not insignificant presence in the West Bank, receives funding and arms from Tehran, and holds identical views about Israelis and Jews. (See the Hamas

---

[1] Oliver Holmes, "Israel launches 'large-scale' attack in Syria after fighter jet crashes." *The Guardian* (UK), February 10, 2018. (https://www.theguardian.com/world/2018/feb/10/israeli-fighter-jet-shot-down-by-syrian-fire-says-military)

[2] Yair Rosenberg, "Did Netanyahu Put Anti-Semitic Words in Hezbollah's Mouth?" *Tablet*, March 9, 2015. (http://www.tabletmag.com/scroll/189519/did-netanyahu-put-anti-semitic-words-in-hezbollahs-mouth)

Clifford D. May   February 14, 2018

Covenant.[3]) Hamas believes that any territory conquered by Muslims must never be surrendered to non-Muslims. This is not a negotiating position. It is a matter of ideology and theology. Hamas has never been and never will be part of a serious peace process.

In this environment, it would require a Palestinian leader of enormous independence, charisma, and courage to negotiate a resolution of the conflict with Israel. Mahmoud Abbas, president of the Palestinian Authority which (loosely) governs the West Bank, is not that leader.

Elected to a four-year term as PA president in 2005, he has remained in that position without benefit of reelection. In recent statements, he made it abundantly clear that he does not accept the basic premise of a two-state solution: two states for two peoples – one of those peoples being the Jewish people.

He does not recognize that the Jewish people has a right to self-determination in any part of its ancient homeland. He recently said that Jerusalem "is Arab, Muslim and Christian"[4] – conspicuously omitting Jerusalem's Jewish roots, implicitly rejecting what historian Barbara Tuchman once pointed out: that Jewish Israelis are living in the same land, speaking the same language, and worshipping the same God as did their ancestors 3,000 years ago. Few peoples can say the same.

It has been years since Mr. Abbas has been willing to sit down and negotiate with Israelis. Instead, he has taken part in a campaign to delegitimize Israel. This includes UN Security Council Resolution 2334,[5] which passed in late 2016 and claimed that Israel has no rights in the eastern sections of Jerusalem – not even the Jewish Quarter of the Old City; not even Judaism's holiest sites, the Western Wall and the Temple Mount. The current administration's recognition of Jerusalem as Israel's capital has at least helped halt the momentum of this damaging narrative.

It is important to understand: This campaign has the strategic intent of justifying attacks against Israel – by Iran, Hezbollah, Hamas, and others – as "resistance" to an "illegitimate regime" that sooner or later is to be fatally poisoned by a cocktail of violence, economic warfare, and diplomacy. So long as that goal appears even remotely realistic, no Palestinian leader can settle for less without painting a target on his back.

Mr. Abbas opposes what he calls "normalization" with Israel, effectively preventing Israelis and Palestinians from working together, getting to know one another, perhaps discovering that they need not be enemies forever.

The BDS campaign – for Boycott, Divestment, and Sanctions – is an integral part of this "anti-normalization" effort. Radical elements play an important role. BDS does not benefit Palestinians.

---

[3] "Hamas Covenant 1988: The Covenant of the Islamic Resistance Movement," *Yale Law School*, August 18, 1988. (http://avalon.law.yale.edu/20th_century/hamas.asp)
[4] Dov Lieber, "US peace envoy blasts Abbas for failure to mention Jerusalem's Jewish connection," *Times of Israel*, Feburary 8, 2018. (https://www.timesofisrael.com/us-peace-envoy-blasts-abbas-for-failure-to-mention-jerusalems-jewish-connection/)
[5] United Nations Security Council, Resolution 2334, December 23, 2016. (http://www.un.org/webcast/pdfs/SRES2334-2016.pdf)

Clifford D. May   February 14, 2018

On the contrary, it is an important cause of the high unemployment and poverty within the West Bank.

In a serious peace process, political leaders on both sides would work toward peaceful coexistence even as negotiations proceeded on borders, security, economic relations, and other issues. That has not been the case in peace processes of the past.

At some point, after Mr. Abbas leaves the scene, a new peace process may be developed. But that will depend on who succeeds Mr. Abbas, on who next leads Palestinians. According to Palestinian Basic Law, Article 37, the Speaker of the Palestinian Legislative Council is to "temporarily" assume the powers and duties of the PA president.[6] Right now, that position is held by a Hamas leader who, according to the Israelis, has been involved in "terrorist activities."

After 60 days, there are to be "free and direct elections to elect a new President." Considering how long it has been since there have been any elections in the West Bank and Gaza, how likely is that? And if balloting fails, if instead – as has been the pattern in the Middle East for centuries – power is taken by force of arms, who is likely to prevail? Hamas? Hezbollah? Other jihadi groups?

I predict with regret: The next Palestinian president will not be Salam Fayyad, the former Palestinian Authority prime minister who, I believe, did contemplate ending the conflict with Israel so as not to sacrifice another generation of Palestinians to the dream of wiping Israel off the map. He also made a serious attempt to build the institutional foundations necessary for the establishment of a Palestinian nation-state that would not be a terrorist-supporting despotism and permanent ward of the international "donor community."

Mr. Fayyad never had broad support on the West Bank or Gaza.[7] Hamas despised him. And, in the end, Mr. Abbas forced Mr. Fayyad out of office. He now lives in the U.S.

Working with Saudi Arabia, the UAE, Egypt, Jordan, and other Sunni Arab partners, as well as any pragmatic elements that can be found within the Palestinian Authority, it may be possible for the administration and Congress to develop a next generation of Palestinian leaders who are serious about resolving the conflict, and who do not see peaceful coexistence with Israel as a euphemism for defeat. But this challenge cannot be overestimated.

I will elaborate on these and other issues and provide recommendations in further testimony below.

Jerusalem: On December 6, 2017, the president announced that it is U.S. policy to recognize Jerusalem as the capital of Israel. This announcement does not predetermine the final status of Jerusalem as decided through bilateral negotiations between Israeli and Palestinians. It does not rule out the possibility of a Palestinian capital in or near eastern Jerusalem. It does, however, recognize reality as well as Israeli sovereignty.

---

[6] The Palestinian Basic Law, Article 37, issued on March 18, 2003, accessed February 12, 2018. (https://www.palestinianbasiclaw.org/basic-law/2003-amended-basic-law)

[7] Clifford D. May. "May: In the West Bank, peace and prosperity are unlikely," *Newsday*, February 6, 2013. (https://www.newsday.com/opinion/oped/in-the-west-bank-peace-and-prosperity-are-unlikely-clifford-d-may-1.4574344)

Clifford D. May												February 14, 2018

I need not remind you that Democratic and Republican members of Congress, by a wide margin, voted for the Jerusalem Embassy Act of 1995 on Oct 24, 1995. It recognizes that Jerusalem is the capital of Israel.[8] The law was adopted by the Senate 93-5, and the House tally was 374-37.[9] The legislation became public law on November 8, 1995. It is fair to say that President Trump has done nothing more than operationalize this overwhelming Congressional sentiment.

Congress expressed this bipartisan sentiment again in 2017. Senate Resolution 176 – a resolution commemorating the 50th anniversary of the reunification of Jerusalem – was approved in the Senate on June 5, 2017.[10] It praised Israel's commitment to religious freedom and its administration of the holy sites in Jerusalem. The resolution reaffirmed: (1) that it is long-standing U.S. bipartisan policy that the permanent status of Jerusalem remains a matter to be decided between the parties through final status negotiations towards a two-state solution; and (2) the Jerusalem Embassy Act of 1995 as U.S. law, and calls upon the president and all U.S. officials to abide by its provisions.[11] The vote was 90-0.

Congressional leaders have been articulate about the need to ensure that U.S. policy recognizes Jerusalem as the capital of Israel. One example: On Oct 24, 1995, Rep. Peter Deutsch, a Florida Democrat, rose "in support of H.R. 1595, which is a piece of legislation that will facilitate a long overdue movement of the United States Embassy in Israel from Tel Aviv to Jerusalem. This is the only Embassy in the world, American Embassy, that is not in the capital that is designated by the country that the Embassy is in."[12]

He added: "[F]ailure to get the two-thirds vote on this bill today would be sending an exactly wrong message because it would be sending a message that there is not resolve in this Congress in support of the peace process and that there is an opening in terms of what could happen in terms of Jerusalem, that the United States Congress has weakened its supports for this peace process."

And Chuck Schumer, then a House member, today Senate Minority leader, noted that whenever "Israel has had control of any portion of Jerusalem, it has been open. The world's holy places have been open. When the Arab nations had control of Jerusalem between 1948 and 1967, no Jew was allowed to visit any of those holy places, and many are important to the Jewish religion, as well as the Christian and Islamic religions. Mr. Speaker, whenever I went to Israel and would have to meet with American officials and leave Jerusalem and go to Tel Aviv, it was embarrassing. It was humiliating. It was wrong. As has been said before, it is a nation's sovereignty to choose its capital. Israel has chosen Jerusalem. It is about time the United States went along."

---

[8] Jerusalem Embassy Act of 1995, Pub. L. 104-45, 109 Stat. 398, codified as amended at 104 U.S.C. (https://www.gpo.gov/fdsys/pkg/PLAW-104publ45/html/PLAW-104publ45.htm)

[9] 141 Cong. Rec. 165 (1995) (https://www.congress.gov/crec/1995/10/24/CREC-1995-10-24.pdf)

[10] 163 Cong. Rec. 95 (2017) (https://www.congress.gov/crec/2017/06/05/CREC-2017-06-05.pdf)

[11] S. Res. 176, 115th Congress (2017). (https://www.congress.gov/115/bills/sres176/BILLS-115sres176ats.pdf)

[12] 141 Cong. Rec. 165 (1995) (https://www.congress.gov/crec/1995/10/24/CREC-1995-10-24.pdf)

Clifford D. May   February 14, 2018

President Trump already has instructed the State Department to begin preparations to move the American Embassy from Tel Aviv to Jerusalem. Recent reports suggest that the move could take place as soon as next year.[13]

Predictably, the announcement led to widespread condemnation of the U.S. by many in the Arab world. The UN Security Council voted to condemn the decision, but Ambassador Nikki Haley cast America's veto.

Some opponents of the announcement warned of catastrophic reactions in what is sometimes called the Muslim world.[14] There were predictions that there would be another *intifada* in Gaza and the West Bank.[15] There were those who attempted to incite such an uprising. But while protests were reported in a number of countries – Jordan, Pakistan, and Malaysia, among them – their size and duration did not live up to the predictions.[16]

In the West Bank, the dominant Fatah party declared three "days of rage" as well as a general strike two days after.[17] On the night of Mr. Trump's address, top Palestinian negotiator Saeb Erekat declared that the two-state solution was now moot and that Palestinians should fight for a one-state outcome.[18] Mr. Abbas called recognition of Jerusalem as Israel's capital a "declaration of the United States' withdrawal from undertaking the role it has played" in the peace process.[19]

Palestinian Aid: The Trump administration has expressed concern about how the Palestinian Authority has been using funding provided by the United States. On January 2, 2018, the administration threatened to cut part of the $700 million in annual aid it provides to the Palestinian Authority.[20] President Trump lamented that despite the hundreds of millions of dollars a year that

---

[13] Mark Landler, "U.S. Presses to Relocate Embassy to Jerusalem by 2019," *The New York Times*, January 18, 2018. (https://www.nytimes.com/2018/01/18/us/politics/trump-israel-embassy-jerusalem.html)

[14] Nahal Toosi, "State Department Warns of Violence Ahead of Trump Jerusalem Decision," *Politico*, December 4. 2017. (https://www.politico.com/story/2017/12/04/trump-israel-jerusalem-violence-279735)

[15] Muhammad Shehada, "Palestinian Rage Over Trump's Jerusalem move Won't Turn into a Third Intifada." *Haaretz* (Israel), December 6, 2017. (https://www.haaretz.com/middle-east-news/.premium-despite-trump-palestinians-won-t-start-a-third-intifada-1.5627898)

[16] Alastair Jamieson, "Trump Jerusalem move sparks more protests across Muslim world." *NBC News*, December 8, 2017. (https://www.nbcnews.com/news/world/trump-jerusalem-move-sparks-more-protests-across-muslim-world-n827626)

[17] Loveday Morris and Ruth Eglash, "Palestinians Clash with Israeli Troops Ahead of 'Day of Rage' at Trump's Jerusalem Move." *The Washington Post*, December 7, 2017. (https://www.washingtonpost.com/world/hamas-calls-for-uprising-as-palestinians-protest-trumps-jerusalem-stance/2017/12/07/eccc91c0-daca-11e7-a241-0848315642d0_story.html?utm_term=.e4133c563e9f)

[18] Noa Landau and Jack Khoury, "'Two-State Solution is Over,' Top Palestinian Diplomat Says After Trump's Jerusalem Speech," *Haaretz* (Israel), December 7, 2017. (https://www.haaretz.com/middle-east-news/palestinians/.premium-two-state-solution-is-over-top-palestinian-diplomat-says-1.5627973)

[19] Adam Rasgon, "Abbas Slams Trump's Jerusalem Move as 'Condemned, Unacceptable.'" *The Jerusalem Post* (Israel), December 6, 2017. (http://www.jpost.com/Arab-Israeli-Conflict/Abbas-slams-Trump-Jerusalem-move-as-condemned-unacceptable-517231)

[20] Anne Gearan "Trump threatens to take away more U.S. aid from Palestinians if they don't negotiate with Israel." *The Washington Post*, January 25, 2018. (https://www.washingtonpost.com/politics/trump-threatens-to-take-away-more-us-aid-from-palestinians-if-they-dont-negotiate-with-israel/2018/01/25/a927e02a-01c3-11e8-8acf-ad2991367d9d_story.html?utm_term=.c92ff94dabfb)

the U.S. puts into Palestinian coffers, the U.S. gets "no appreciation or respect."[21] He further stated: "They don't even want to negotiate a long overdue ... peace treaty with Israel." Palestinian officials responded by calling Mr. Trump "not a serious man."[22] Abbas advisor Ahmed Majdalani reportedly said: "[W]e will sever all ties with the Americans," and "this means the end of the peace process and the U.S. role there."[23]

Since this initial exchange between the administration and the Palestinian Authority, the White House has withheld $60 million in assistance to the United Nations Relief Works Agency (UNRWA), which is the primary vehicle for administering aid to Palestinians in refugee camps across the region.[24] More on that immediately below.

Congress also has been expressing opposition to the PA's continuing incitement to terrorism and celebration of terrorists. The Taylor Force Act,[25] named after the U.S. Army veteran who was murdered by a Palestinian in 2016 while on a visit to Israel, would require the PA to take tangible steps to condemn violence and to stop providing salaries to terrorists imprisoned after having attacked Americans and Israelis. The House of Representatives passed the legislation unanimously. The bill has not yet been brought to a vote in the Senate. Congress should support such accountability and transparency as a requirement for the foreign aid it provides. Taxpayer dollars should not be used by the PA to encourage or reward terrorism.

UNRWA: The administration's decision to withhold part of the assistance it provides to UNRWA has further infuriated the PA. The Palestinians apparently view American payments to UNRWA as an entitlement. The administration views such payments as charitable giving by American taxpayers.

Among the largest impediments to a workable two-state solution is the growing number of Palestinians that have been granted refugee status by UNRWA. Since 1950, when UNWRA began operations, the number of Palestinians claiming refugee status has risen from approximately 800,000 to more than 5 million.

Of course, nearly 70 years after the 1948 war, we know that the vast majority of those UNRWA calls refugees are nothing of the kind. Rather, they are descendants of refugees – children, grandchildren, and even great grandchildren who have been kept in a perpetual state of dependency, subsisting on international welfare with the false hope that one day they will be settled in Israel which, given their numbers, will then become a Palestinian-majority state.

[21] Zeke Miller and Jill Colvin, "Trump Threatens to Cut Off US Aid to Palestinian Authority," *Associated Press*, January 3, 2018. (https://www.apnews.com/014cfbb86511429d9c09c818a76f58c0)

[22] Adam Rasgon, "Abbas Adviser: Trump's Twitter Storm on Aid Has Absolutely No Justification," *The Jerusalem Post* (Israel), January 3, 2017. (http://www.jpost.com/Arab-Israeli-Conflict/Abbas-adviser-Trumps-Twitter-storm-on-aid-has-absolutely-no-justification-532695)

[23] Grant Rumley, "Mahmoud Abbas Doesn't Have a Trump Strategy," *Foreign Policy*, January 3, 2017. (http://foreignpolicy.com/2018/01/03/mahmoud-abbas-doesnt-have-a-trump-strategy/)

[24] Anne Gearan, "Trump threatens to take away more U.S. aid from Palestinians if they don't negotiate with Israel," *The Washington Post*, January 25, 2018. (https://www.washingtonpost.com/politics/trump-threatens-to-take-away-more-us-aid-from-palestinians-if-they-dont-negotiate-with-israel/2018/01/25/a927c02a-01c3-11e8-8acf-ad2991367d9d_story.html?utm_term=.c92ff94dabfb)

[25] Taylor Force Act, H.R. 1164, 115th Congress (2017). (https://www.congress.gov/115/bills/hr1164/BILLS-115hr1164pcs.pdf)

UNRWA's former general counsel James Lindsay has acknowledged that "[i]n truth, the vast majority of UNRWA's registered refugees have already been "resettled" or "reintegrated" and that the "only thing preventing all of these citizens from ceasing to be "refugees" is UNRWA's unique definition of what constitutes a refugee."[26]

If UNRWA continues its practice of designating the descendants of refugees as refugees, there will be an estimated 14.7 million Palestinian "refugees" by 2050.[27] That exceeds Israel's current population of 8 million,[28] with minorities – the largest being Arab Muslims – currently constituting as much as 25 percent.

The UN High Commissioner for Refugees, which deals with all non-Palestinian refugees around the world, does not award refugee status to the descendants of refugees. The UNRWA definition has no non-political logic. That said, utilizing the UNHCR definition of refugee does not imply the U.S. should cease assisting impoverished Palestinians with the goal of helping them become productive and self-supporting (a goal UNRWA has not seriously attempted to achieve).

The UNRWA claims to serve 2.1 million Palestinian refugees in Jordan, 1.3 million in Gaza, 800,000 in the West Bank, 543,000 in Syria, and 463,000 in Lebanon. The UNRWA operates 702 schools, 143 healthcare facilities, and overall operates 1,118 facilities. UNRWA is staffed by close to 31,000 local employees plus 178 international staff.[29] By contrast, the UNHCR operates with a 10,000-person staff serving millions upon millions of refugees around the world.

The UNRWA has grown into a massive self-sustaining bureaucracy that allows the Palestinian Authority to shirk its responsibilities to provide basic services to its own people in the West Bank and Gaza and delays the permanent integration of millions into neighboring Arab states.

The agency's overall inefficiency and extraordinarily high administrative costs make the UNRWA – as currently constructed - a dubious investment for American taxpayers. At the very least, its brazen use of the descendants of refugees as pawns in a war of attrition against Israel does not deserve American support. How America spends its limited foreign assistance matters. Aiding impoverished Palestinians through aid programs has merit, but policies that do not serve the long-term interests of the United States while impeding any serious peace process ought to be reconsidered.

This reminder: In the late 1940s and 1950s, the number of Jews forced from Arab and Muslim countries was about the same as the number of Palestinians (as noted above, roughly 800,000) who

---

[26] Asaf Romirowsky and Alexander Joffe, "The True Obstacle to Peace Between Israelis and Palestinians," *Forbes*, March 26, 2013. (https://www.forbes.com/sites/realspin/2013/03/26/the-true-obstacle-to-peace-between-israelis-and-palestinians/#fabbe1953f0d)

[27] Jonathan Schanzer, "Defining Palestinian refugee status and the consequences," *The Hill*, May 22, 2012. (http://thehill.com/blogs/congress-blog/foreign-policy/228877-defining-palestinian-refugee-status-and-the-consequences)

[28] Central Intelligence Agency, "The World Factbook," accessed February 12, 2018. (https://www.cia.gov/library/publications/the-world-factbook/geos/is.html)

[29] United Nations Relief Works Agency, "in figures," January 1, 2017. (https://www.unrwa.org/sites/default/files/content/resources/unrwa_in_figures_2017_english.pdf)

fled from what became Israel. Not one of the Jews exiled from those Middle Eastern countries – in which their families had lived for millennia – remains a refugee today. Nor are any demanding a "right of return" to their birthplaces in Arab and Muslim countries.

The need for change is clear. That has to mean the gradual transition of ersatz refugees to post-refugee status. Arab states should absorb and grant citizenship to those who for generations have lived within their territories. In the areas governed by the Palestinian Authority, new infrastructure and government institutions will be needed for PA leaders to finally take responsibility for those under their control.

Congress has been talking about UNRWA reform for years with little to show for it. Over the last decade, congressional initiatives to audit UNRWA's expenditures, crack down on the use of UNRWA facilities by terrorists, and remove anti-Semitic textbooks from UNRWA schools have had little effect. To be sure, pushing back against the inertia of a 70-year-old bureaucracy that lives to perpetuate and expand a refugee crisis is an up-hill battle – particularly when the Department of State has too often in the past defended the status quo while ignoring the underlying problems.

With that in mind, the administration's recent decision to withhold funds from the UNRWA marks an opportunity that Congress would be wise to seize. The elected representatives of American taxpayers should take the lead in reforming this wayward agency. And with a U.S. ambassador to the United Nations for the first time opening the door to UNRWA oversight and reform, now is the time for Congress to work collaboratively with the administration to make changes long overdue.

UN Reform: The administration is working to mute the anti-Israel drumbeat at Turtle Bay. One priority has been to mitigate the damage done by UNSCR 2334,[30] which the Obama administration declined to veto, and which calls upon UN member states to differentiate between the territory of the State of Israel and the territory that fell to Israel in 1967 when it fought a defensive war against its Arab neighbors. That the Six-Day War was defensive is indisputable.

Then-Egyptian President Gamel Abdel Nasser declared at the time that the grievance he intended to address was the "existence of Israel." He promised that the war would result in "Israel's destruction." Cairo radio declared Israel would be "liquidated." Syrian dictator Hafiz al-Assad – father of Syria's current dictator, Bashar al-Assad – vowed "a battle of annihilation." Then-Iraqi President Abdul Rahman Aref said the opportunity must be seized "to wipe Israel off the map … to wipe out the ignominy which has been with us since 1948." Ahmed Shukairy, a representative of the then three-year-old Palestine Liberation Organization, was asked what would happen to Israelis after the war. "I estimate that none of them will survive," he said.[31]

Israel seized Gaza from Egypt, then the occupying power. It seized the West Bank from Jordan, then the occupying power there. Prior to those occupations, the West Bank – previously known as Judea and Samaria – had been ruled by the British Empire and, for centuries before that, by the

---

[30] United Nations Security Council, Resolution 2334, December 23, 2016.
(http://www.un.org/webcast/pdfs/SRES2334-2016.pdf)
[31] Clifford D. May, "Unhappy Anniversary," *National Review*, June 14, 2007.
(http://www.nationalreview.com/article/221280/unhappy-anniversary-clifford-d-may)

Ottoman Empire. Never have these or any other territories constituted anything resembling a Palestinian state. Through negotiations with Israelis, the opportunity to create such a state could be opened for the first time in history. In return, however, Palestinians need to resolve their conflict with the Jewish state.

UNSCR 2334 calls the Israeli presence in eastern Jerusalem a violation of international law. Included within eastern Jerusalem: the Jewish Quarter of the Old City and the most ancient and holy sites of the Jewish people: the Western Wall, or Kotel, and the Temple Mount. During and immediately after Israel's War of Independence, Jordanian forces expelled Jews from those areas and destroyed or desecrated Jewish holy sites.

It is virtually impossible to repeal a UNSC resolution. The administration's recognition of Jerusalem as Israel's capital at least makes clear that the U.S. regards the resolution as based on an unfair and biased reading of history and international law – as by any objective measure it is.

The U.S. Congress, to its credit, opposed UNSCR 2334. Legislators condemned it immediately. Still, it remains in place and continues to provide fodder for anti-Israelism and anti-Semitism at the United Nations and beyond.

U.S. Ambassador to the UN Nikki Haley has repeatedly called for an end to the river of resolutions condemning Israel, fast flowing even at a time when the Middle East is engulfed in far more lethal crises: hundreds of thousands of Syrians killed and millions turned into refugees; Egypt at war with jihadis in Sinai; a devastating civil war in Yemen – the list goes on. About these crises, the UN says little and does less.

Ambassador Haley has threatened to cut aid to the United Nations over actions taken in the General Assembly to condemn U.S. recognition of Jerusalem as Israel's capital. In December, Ambassador Haley announced that the U.S. had negotiated a $285 reduction to the UN's coffers.

BDS: Boycott, Divestment, and Sanctions activities represent another impediment to normalization and, not just incidentally, to the possibility of Palestinians building a viable economy. Joint ventures, economic manufacturing zones, and the making and growing of products for export have empowered Palestinians and provided much-needed jobs, more often than not, averaging two to four times the wages offered at the small number of Palestinian factories.[32] BDS supporters, however, have attempted to isolate these companies and intimidate those who attempt to foster such interactions.

One example: Daniel Birnbaum is an Israeli entrepreneur, the founder of the international company SodaStream, which manufactures devices that let you turn tap water into sparkling water.

---

[32] Devin Leonard and Yaacov Benmelch, "How SodaStream Makes—and Markets—Peace," *Bloomberg Businessweek*, December 20, 2017. (https://www.bloomberg.com/news/features/2017-12-20/how-sodastream-makes-and-markets-peace); Ali Sawafta. "For many Palestinians, Israel settlement work the only option." *Reuters*, February 22, 2016. (https://www.reuters.com/article/us-israel-palestinians-workers/for-many-palestinians-israel-settlement-work-the-only-option-idUSKCN0VV1J6)

Clifford D. May   February 14, 2018

In an interview a few years ago, he told me that one day he had an idea: He wanted to "employ Palestinians."

So he bought a factory on the West Bank – where unemployment runs about 30 percent – and he hired more than 500 Palestinians. He also hired 350 Israeli Arabs and 300 Israeli Jews. He paid them all "Israeli wages," roughly four times higher than the West Bank average. Because Palestinians are not Israeli citizens and therefore do not qualify for Israeli health care, he purchased private insurance for them, as well as for their dependents, knowing full well that "each employee supports about ten family members."[33]

For a while he thought he was succeeding: He was producing a good product and providing good jobs for Palestinians and most important for him, he was demonstrating that it is possible for Israelis and Arabs, Muslims and Jews, men and women, to work together, respect each other and even learn to like one another.

Of course, the BDS campaign was soon accusing him of stealing land and "profiting from the occupation." That was among the reasons his factory in the West Bank was eventually shut down. Efforts by BDS activists have resulted in the loss of thousands of other Palestinian jobs. Leaders of BDS organizations oppose the very existence of Israel. They seek to persuade students on college campuses that Israel is an "apartheid" regime – even as they do everything they can to separate Israelis and Palestinians, to keep them from developing anything resembling normal relations between neighbors.

One of the key BDS organizations operating in the U.S. is American Muslims for Palestine (AMP). It orchestrates BDS campaigns aimed at delegitimizing and waging economic warfare against the State of Israel.

Several individuals now working for or on behalf of AMP once worked for or on behalf of the Holy Land Foundation for Relief and Development (HLF), the Islamic Association for Palestine (IAP), and/or KindHearts for Charitable Development. All three organizations were implicated by the federal government for financing the Hamas, a designated terrorist group, between 2001 and 2011. Moreover, several of AMP's donors were involved in organizations implicated in funding Hamas, Palestinian Islamic Jihad, and even al-Qaeda.[34]

The Blacklist: On March 24, 2016, the United Nations Human Rights Council voted to create a blacklist of companies that operate in the Golan Heights, the West Bank, and eastern Jerusalem. Thirty-two nations voted in favor of creating such a database. Fifteen countries abstained from the vote, including some members of the European Union.[35]

---

[33] Clifford D. May. "Jobless and desperate Palestinians," *The Washington Times*, October 27, 2015. (https://www.washingtontimes.com/news/2015/oct/27/clifford-may-jobless-and-desperate-palestinians/)

[34] Jonathan Schanzer "Examining Current Terrorist Financing Trends and the Threat to the Homeland," *Congressional Testimony before the House Homeland Security Committee Counterterrorism and Intelligence Subcommittee*, May 12, 2016. (http://docs.house.gov/meetings/HM/HM05/20160512/104904/HHRG-114-HM05-Wstate-SchanzerJ-20160512.pdf)

[35] United Nations Human Rights Council. Resolution 31/36, "Israeli settlements in the Occupied Palestinian Territory, including East Jerusalem, and in the occupied Syrian Golan." April 20, 2016. (https://documents-dds-ny.un.org/doc/UNDOC/GEN/G16/082/57/PDF/G1608257.pdf?OpenElement)

Clifford D. May												February 14, 2018

On January 26, 2018, the United Nations Human Rights Council released an interim report that highlighted the actions taken to investigate companies operating in these territories. The UN identified 206 companies that it believes may be operating in these areas. So far, the UNHRC has contacted 64 in an attempt to ascertain their companies' involvement in these territories.

The report did not name specific companies but rather indicated the number of entities it was pursuing and where those organizations were domiciled. The report indicated that 143 companies included in the list were based in Israel, while 22 were situated in the U.S., with an additional 7 companies operating from Germany.

Israel is an attractive place for investors because of its dynamic high tech sector and start-up culture. But the list is meant to have a chilling effect on the Israeli economy. It represents yet another example of UN bias and discrimination. Israelis are willing to help Palestinians achieve self-determination and a sustainable economy – if Palestinians are willing to peacefully coexist with Israelis. Keep in mind: The Chinese are not willing to do the same for Tibetans, the Russians are not willing to do the same for Chechens, nor will any Middle Eastern country do the same for the Kurds – to name just three examples. Yet the UN has no interest in the aspirations of these stateless nations, and no interest in criticizing those who oppress them. The double standard could hardly be more obvious and egregious.

Palestinian Leadership: The rhetoric from Palestinian leaders in response to the administration's policies can be characterized as combative. "America can no longer be the steward of the peace process on its own. We have had enough of that," declared Mahmoud Abbas' advisor, Nabil Sha'ath.[36] In addition, the Palestinian leadership announced it would seek recognition in more international bodies, it appealed to the International Criminal Court (ICC) to start a "judicial inquiry into Israeli settlements," and declared that it was reconsidering its recognition of Israel.[37]

This so-called recognition is misleading. Israel is not recognized by Palestinian leaders as the homeland of the Jewish people. Furthermore, their demand that there be a "right of return" for millions of Palestinian "refugees" is intended to turn Israel into an Arab/Muslim majority state, where Jewish Israelis would become a minority. It is unlikely they would be a minority with equal rights. In no Arab/Muslim majority country today do minorities enjoy anything close to equal rights. By contrast, Israel's many minorities – Arabs, Muslims, Christians, Druze, etc. – enjoy rights and freedoms unavailable anywhere else in the region.

---

[36] Adam Rasgon, "Abbas Advisor: U.S. Can Play Role in Multilateral Peace Process," *The Jerusalem Post* (Israel), December 11, 2017. (http://www.jpost.com/American-Politics/Palestinian-advisor-US-can-play-role-in-multilateral-peace-process-517661)
[37] Jack Khoury, "Abbas Declares Oslo Accords Dead: 'Trump's Peace Plan is a Slap, We'll Slap Back,'" *Haaretz* (Israel), January 15, 2018. (https://www.haaretz.com/middle-east-news/palestinians/abbas-declares-oslo-accords-dead-trump-s-peace-plan-is-a-slap-1.5730759); "PLO says it will seek action in UNSC, General Assembly and ICC," *Wafa News Agency* (Palestinian Territories), February 3, 2018.
(http://english.wafa.ps/page.aspx?id=ncLYdHa96338342166ancLYdH); "PLO to study revoking its recognition of Israel," *Middle East Eye*, February 3, 2018. (http://www.middleeasteye.net/news/plo-study-revoking-its-recognition-israel-690429165)

Clifford D. May												February 14, 2018

In recent weeks, the Palestinian position on American mediation appears to have softened. Palestinian officials are now saying they would accept an American role in the peace process so long as other international actors are involved.[38] However, it is unclear whether those actors would be acceptable to Israel. Just days after President Trump's speech, Mr. Abbas said the Palestinians would join more than 20 international organizations, pledging he would sign on to one every consecutive Monday.[39] But nearly two months later, he has not followed through. Instead, however, he has taken to deploying vitriolic language and anti-Semitic tropes.

In a strange and disturbing speech before the Palestinian Central Council on January 14, Mr. Abbas lambasted Israel and Zionism for over two hours. He blamed the problems of the Palestinians on everyone from Oliver Cromwell to Napoleon Bonaparte to Winston Churchill.[40] He dismissed the Jewish connection to the land of Israel, insisting that the Jewish state is a "colonial project that has nothing to do with Judaism."[41]

This was not his first descent into serious anti-Semitism: Just this past December, at the Organization of Islamic Cooperation summit in Turkey, he accused Jews of "faking and counterfeiting history and religion."[42] In 2016, Abbas accused Israeli rabbis of poisoning Palestinian water wells during a speech to the European parliament.[43] And recall his PhD thesis, which played down the number of Jewish victims of the Holocaust and suggested an alliance between Zionists and Nazis.[44]

Nevertheless, it was an astonishing performance for a man once heralded by many as a moderate and a peacemaker.[45] Mr. Abbas' recent comments and actions make clear that he is not a viable partner for any peace process. As President Obama's former ambassador to Israel, Daniel Shapiro,

---

[38] "Arabs seek 'multilateral' process to revive mideast peace talks." *The Daily Star* (Lebanon), February 3, 2018. (http://www.thedailystar.net/backpage/arabs-seek-multilateral-process-revive-mideast-peace-talks-1529098)

[39] Ben Lynfield, "Abbas Says Palestinians to Seek Full United Nations Membership," *The Jerusalem Post* (Israel), December 19, 2017. (http://www.jpost.com/Israel-News/Abbas-says-Palestinians-to-seek-full-UN-membership-518442)

[40] "Mahmoud Abbas: The PLO Should Reexamine its Agreements with Israel; We Will No Longer Accept the U.S. as Mediator," *Middle East Media Research Institute*, January 14, 2018. (https://www.memri.org/tv/mahmoud-abbas-plo-should-reexamine-agreements-with-israel-we-will-not-accept-america-as-mediator/transcript)

[41] Dov Lieber, "Rewriting History, Abbas Calls Israel a 'Colonial Project' Unrelated to Judaism," *The Times of Israel*, January 15, 2018. (https://www.timesofisrael.com/rewriting-history-abbas-calls-israel-a-colonial-project-unrelated-to-judaism/)

[42] Yair Rosenberg, "Palestinian President Accuses Jews of 'Counterfeiting History and Religion,' Claims Qur'an Says they 'Fabricate Truth'," *Tablet*, December 14, 2017. (http://www.tabletmag.com/scroll/251604/palestinian-president-accuses-jews-of-counterfeiting-history-and-religion-claims-quran-says-they-fabricate-truth)

[43] Robin Emmott and Dan Williams, "Abbas says some Israeli rabbis called for poisoning Palestinian water," *Reuters*, June 23, 2016. (https://www.reuters.com/article/us-palestinians-israel/abbas-says-some-israeli-rabbis-called-for-poisoning-palestinian-water-idUSKCN0Z91J8)

[44] Ronen Bergman, "Abbas' book reveals: The 'Nazi-Zionist plot' of the Holocaust," *YNet News* (Israel), November 26, 2014. (https://www.ynetnews.com/articles/0,7340,L-4596121,00.html)

[45] Grant Rumley, "The Tragedy of Mahmoud Abbas," *The Atlantic*, January 21, 2018. (https://www.theatlantic.com/international/archive/2018/01/mahmoud-abbas-palestine-israel-speech/551072/)

Clifford D. May   February 14, 2018

stated after the speech: "[T]he United States must conclude that there is no reason to believe Abbas has it within him to take the necessary decisions to reach a peace deal with Israel."[46]

Recently, Jason Greenblatt, President Trump's chief envoy to the Middle East peace process, addressed Mr. Abbas in a series of tweets. "Pres. Abbas states about Jerusalem: 'it is Arab, Muslim, and Christian,' and makes no mention of any Jewish ties. Nothing peaceful or productive can come from statements like this."[47]

He added: "Lasting peace will not be achieved by denying Judaism's thousands of years of ties to Jerusalem. Jerusalem is holy to Muslims, Christians, and Jews. Peace can ONLY be based on truth, and what [President Trump] said is the truth: 'Jerusalem is today, and must remain, a place where Jews pray at the Western Wall, where Christians walk the Stations of the Cross, and where Muslims worship at Al-Aqsa Mosque.'"

Congress should now give serious consideration to what will follow Mr. Abbas who, at 82, is in the 13th year of his four-year elected term in office. A succession crisis is coming. A leadership crisis is already here.

The Future of the Peace Process: If there is to be a revived peace process, the next Palestinian leader will need to do what Mr. Abbas did not do: begin to prepare the Palestinian people for peaceful coexistence. That means promoting tolerance, not inciting hatred and violence against Israelis and Jews, not opposing efforts to "normalize" relations between Israelis and Palestinians, and exploring economic cooperation.

It means telling Palestinians that peace will require difficult compromises, that the extermination of Israel is no longer the goal, that the Jews will not be driven out of Jerusalem, and that there is a Jewish people who have lived in the Middle East for thousands of years, and who have a right to self-determination in part of their ancient homeland.

Once a majority of Palestinians embrace these views, the peace process will proceed rapidly toward the desired end. However, so long as Palestinian leaders and a majority of Palestinians regard compromise with Israelis and acceptance of the Jewish state as defeat, the peace process is certain to lead nowhere – as it has in the past.

Much depends on who succeeds Mr. Abbas. But establishing a reliable succession process is one of the many nation-building tasks he failed to tackle during his years in power.

There are other impediments to peace. As noted above, Hamas remains a strong force and Hamas rejects the very idea of Palestinians living in peace alongside a Jewish state. Its intentions are

---

[46] Daniel Shapiro, "Abbas Exits with One Final, Outrageous Performance. Now, America Must Contain the Damage," *Haaretz* (Israel), January 17, 2018. (https://www.haaretz.com/opinion/.premium-after-abbas-outrageous-exit-america-must-contain-the-damage-1.5730854)

[47] Michael Wilner, "Greenblatt Criticizes Abbas' Statement on Jerusalem's Holy Status," *The Jerusalem Post* (Israel), February 8, 2018. (http://www.jpost.com/Arab-Israeli-Conflict/Greenblatt-enters-war-of-words-with-Abbas-breaking-diplomatic-silence-542104?utm_source=dlvr.it&utm_medium=twitter)

candidly annihilationist and genocidal. It continues to spend international aid money building rockets to fire into Israeli cities and constructing tunnels so that terrorists can invade Israeli towns.

Changing Regional Architecture: Relations between Israel and several of its Sunni/Arab neighbors have been improving. Driving this détente: the common threat posed by the Islamic Republic. The Saudis and Emiratis in particular appear to recognize that security cooperation with Israel is essential if Tehran is to be kept at bay.

At the same time, Israel is actively assisting Egypt in Sinai where jihadis have been waging a terrorist war. Israel's military and intelligence cooperation with the Hashemite Kingdom of Jordan is essential to that country's security as well.

Israel's capabilities in cyber warfare, agriculture, and the science of producing clean and abundant fresh water could benefit all its neighbors.[48]

It is useful for Congress to encourage rapprochement in every way possible. That said, I think we can expect only incremental improvements at this juncture. The Saudis and Emiratis cannot afford to be accused by Tehran of betraying the Palestinian cause. Iran's mullahs are only too eager to call the Saudis Zionists. Keep in mind that the Islamic Republic's position on Israel is identical to that of Hezbollah, Hamas, al-Qaeda, and the Islamic State: no conflict resolution, no peaceful coexistence – only a jihad to exterminate the Jewish state.

Wall Street Journal columnist Yaroslav Trofimov recently noted that "any Saudi opening to Israel is guaranteed to be exploited by the kingdom's rivals, and may even include a boycott of the hajj, or pilgrimage, to Mecca, a senior Saudi official cautioned."[49]

"Palestine is not an easy issue," he quoted the official as saying. "Saudi Arabia is expecting to hold Islamic leadership, and will not let it go easily. And, if you need Israel in anything, you can do it anyway, without having a relationship."

Still, with at least some of Israel's neighbors no longer eager to see the Jewish state wiped off the map, there is a glimmer of hope that Israelis and Palestinians can eventually find their way toward peaceful coexistence, even as terrible sectarian wars rage throughout much of their region. While the Palestinian-Israeli conflict cannot, I believe, be solved anytime soon, much can be done to stabilize the situation and prepare for opportunities that may arise in the future.

Such preparation will require significant work on the part of both Congress and the administration. But if Americans do not shoulder this responsibility, no one else will.

With this as background, permit me to suggest a few ideas and actions.

---

[48] Clifford D. May, "Unexpected miracle in the Holy Land," *The Washington Times*, December 1, 2015. (https://www.washingtontimes.com/news/2015/dec/1/clifford-may-water-in-israel/)

[49] Yaroslav Trofimov, "For Saudis and Israelis, Cost of Open Ties Outweighs the Benefits," *The Wall Street Journal*, February 1, 2018. (https://www.wsj.com/articles/for-sandis-and-israelis-cost-of-open-ties-outweighs-the-benefits-1517481001)

Clifford D. May   February 14, 2018

Policy Recommendations:

- Congress should demand that the State Department declassify a congressionally mandated report that exposes UNRWA's underlying myth – so that taxpayers can finally know how much of their funds actually support refugees from 1948 and how much are disguised welfare payments to Palestinians who should be helped instead to find productive employment in an economy not indefinitely dependent on America and other members of the "international donor community."

- Congress should insist on an independent audit of the UNRWA. As the major funder, the U.S. has the right to know how American taxpayer money is being spent. The UN will resist, but Congress should insist – establishing clear benchmarks for continued funding and laying out a timeline for transitioning UNRWA services to the Palestinian Authority, host-nation Arab states, and the UN High Commissioner for Refugees, the office in charge of all refugees except Palestinians.

- Congress should review the definition of "refugee" used by the UNRWA, which currently includes the descendants of refugees and has exacerbated the problem and will continue to do so over the years ahead. A definition based on the actual number of refugees would make conflict resolution much more achievable.

- Congress needs to begin the long-overdue process of serious reform at the UN. The United Nations Human Rights Council along with the UNRWA and other UN bodies are inciting hatred against Israel and passing reams of biased resolutions condemning Israel while ignoring the egregious human rights abuses being committed by the world's worst human rights violators – Iran, North Korea, Syria, Venezuela, Russia, China, and Cuba among them.

- Congress should take action to require greater economic transparency and integrity at the UN. American funding should depend on results.

- Congress should pass the bipartisan Israel Anti-Boycott Act.[50] This legislation would make implementation of the UNHRC blacklist of Israeli companies illegal under U.S. law and reaffirm that boycotts of this nature run afoul of the U.S. Export Administration Act. The legislation also would require the Export Import Bank to consider whether an entity complies with BDS when evaluating potential credit applications.

- BDS groups operate on college campuses in the U.S. and promote commercial boycotts of Israel in many U.S. states. Twenty-five states have enacted laws or executive orders opposing boycotts of Israel. Congress should support these efforts by passing the bipartisan Combatting BDS Act,[51] which would provide states additional legal protections to reject boycotts of Israel.

---

[50] Israel Anti-Boycott Act, S. 720, 115th Congress (2017). (https://www.congress.gov/115/bills/s720/BILLS-115s720is.pdf)

[51] Combating BDS Act of 2017, S. 170, 115th Congress (2017). (https://www.congress.gov/115/bills/s170/BILLS-115s170is.pdf)

- Congress should pass the Taylor Force Act.[52] The act passed the House but has not yet been brought to a vote in the Senate. The legislation would limit funds to the Palestinian Authority if it continues to pay terrorists salaries after they are captured, prosecuted, convicted, and imprisoned in Israel. The legislation also would restrict aid if the Palestinian Authority does not take steps to end violence against American and Israeli citizens. Congress should support such accountability as a requirement for the foreign aid it provides.

- The administration, with congressional support, should attempt to work with Saudi Arabia, the UAE, and other Sunni Arab partners, as well any pragmatic elements within the Palestinian Authority, to create a leadership succession plan, one that will empower Palestinian leaders who are open to conflict resolution and do not see peaceful coexistence with Israel as tantamount to defeat. Without such a plan in place, the possibility of chaos, violence and instability following Mr. Abbas' passing looms large.

- A two-state solution implies two states for two peoples – one of those people being the Jewish people. The Palestinian side must accept that premise prior to negotiations in pursuit of a two-state solution. The theory that acceptance of that premise will emerge at the end of talks has failed in the past and is likely to fail in the future.

- In a revived peace process, the U.S. should insist that political leaders on both sides take active steps toward normalization of relations and peaceful coexistence even as negotiations proceed on borders, security, economic relations, and other issues. This, too, has not been the practice in past peace processes.

- In September 2016, the Obama administration reached a Memorandum of Understanding (MOU) with Israel guaranteeing $38 billion over a ten-year period from FY 2019 to FY 2028. The memorandum would give Israel $33 billion in Foreign Military Financing (FMF) and an additional $5 billion in missile defense assistance. The funds are to be allocated in $3.8 billion increments annually.[53] The agreement handcuffs the ability of Congress to appropriate funds for Israel above the $3.8 billion level. The Israeli government agreed in a letter to return any additional funds that Congress provided for two years.[54] Congress should have the ability and flexibility to provide funds to Israel should it decide Israel needs additional resources to defend itself from the Islamic Republic and other enemies. Israel also should have the ability to use the funds for fuel in emergency situations rather than strictly limiting the funds to FMF and missile defense resources. Congress has appropriated

---

[52] Taylor Force Act, H.R. 1164, 115th Congress (2017). (https://www.congress.gov/115/bills/hr1164/BILLS-115hr1164pcs.pdf)

[53] The White House, Press Release, "FACT SHEET: Memorandum of Understanding Reached with Israel," September 14, 2016. (https://obamawhitehouse.archives.gov/the-press-office/2016/09/14/fact-sheet-memorandum-understanding-reached-israel)

[54] Josh Rogin, "Obama and Israel cut Congress out of the aid game." *The Washington Post*, September 14, 2016. (https://www.washingtonpost.com/news/josh-rogin/wp/2016/09/14/obama-and-israel-cut-congress-out-of-the-aid-game/?utm_term=.574a0b57cee2)

an additional $75 million for Israel above the $3.8 billion in the latest appropriations bill.[55] Congress should continue to exercise its appropriations powers to provide Israel with assistance within the terms of the MOU and beyond, if necessary.

- Congress should support the transfer of the U.S. Embassy to Jerusalem without delay.

- Congress and the administration should recognize Israel's sovereignty over the Golan Heights, as FDD has previously suggested.[56]

Madam Chairman, Ranking Member Deutch, thank you again for the opportunity to testify today. If I have missed any issues you wish to cover, please let me know. I look forward to your questions.

---

[55] Michael Wilner, "Trump Supports $75M. Additional Aid to Israel Beyond Obama-Era MOU," *The Jerusalem Post* (Israel), September 11, 2017. (http://www.jpost.com/Israel-News/Trump-supports-75m-supplemental-aid-to-Israel-beyond-Obama-era-MOU-504800)
[56] Jonathan Schanzer and Mark Dubowitz, "Standing With Israel on the Golan Heights," *The Wall Street Journal*, February 16, 2017. (https://www.wsj.com/articles/standing-with-israel-on-the-golan-heights-1487272241)

Ms. Ros-Lehtinen. Thank you so much, sir.

Mr. al-Omari.

STATEMENT OF MR. GHAITH AL-OMARI, SENIOR FELLOW, IRWIN LEVY FAMILY PROGRAM ON THE U.S.-ISRAEL STRATEGIC RELATIONSHIP, THE WASHINGTON INSTITUTE FOR NEAR EAST POLICY

Mr. al-Omari. Thank you very much, Madam Chairman, Ranking Member, esteemed members. It is an honor to be here.

The administration seems intent on presenting a peace plan. There has been a lot of speculation, particularly in the Arab press. The reality is we do not know what is in this peace plan. It is being held very close in a very small circle.

Yet I would submit that, no matter what the peace plan looks like, no matter how balanced, no matter how well thought through, right now it is going to fail. And it is going to fail because of domestic politics among Palestinians, Israelis, and the region.

In Israel, the coalition of Prime Minister Netanyahu very strongly constricts his ability to make decisions. His legal troubles, that we saw yesterday, do not make things easier.

On the Palestinian side, President Abbas has a 30-percent approval rating. Seventy percent of the Palestinians want him to leave. He is not a leader who is capable of making the difficult decisions that we need to see.

The decisions by the administration on Jerusalem in particular but also UNRWA have complicated things for the Palestinians and for the Arab states.

For the Palestinians, as a matter of principle and as a matter of political expedience, Abbas thought that he has to take a hardline position. Some of the policies he is adopting are questionable. Some of the statements that he made are unacceptable, especially those that deny the Jewish connection to the land. Yet he is in a difficult position.

On the Arab side, the Jerusalem decision, in particular, has diminished the ability of Arab states to pressure and to leverage the Palestinians because they have to be seen on the same side of this issue.

All of this does not bode well for the success of a peace process. And failure in this particular case comes with a price, particularly seeing how tense things are on the ground. This price could be a price in terms of security and a price in terms of the potential collapse of the P.A.—in no one's interest.

That said, I do not believe that it is a wise approach to totally neglect the peace process. Instead, the administration needs to have less ambitious objectives that are achievable. In particular, I think there are four areas that need to be focused on.

One, and the foremost and most important, is security. Security and security cooperation between the Palestinians and the Israelis is probably one of the very few success stories we have seen from that region over the last few years. We saw it in action only this last weekend. The Palestinian security forces, under American support, have become professional, reliable partners by the admission of Israeli security leaders. We need to continue doing this. Specifically, we need to continue directly supporting the Palestinian security forces and the Office of the U.S. Security Coordinator, the three-star general, who has been doing a fantastic job in supporting security and security cooperation.

Second, the West Bank. Things in the West Bank are tense. Emotions are high. Things are volatile. Luckily, because of the security cooperation, the Israeli defense establishment has actually conceptualized a number of projects to support the West Bank. Many of these projects, though, got stuck in Israeli internal political wranglings. We should engage Israel to see how we can apply some of these particular projects, approved and suggested by the IDF, particularly when it comes to Palestinian access to Area C and to giving Palestinians more building and zoning rights around urban Palestinian areas.

Three, Gaza. Gaza is—the situation there is, from a humanitarian point of view, unconscionable. This could lead to a war. Ideally, aid to Gaza should come through the Palestinian Authority. However, reconciliation has failed, and it is likely to fail in the foreseeable future.

So, in the immediate term, I think there are three things that need to be done. A, we directly and through our allies should pressure the Palestinian Authority to remove some of the punitive measures they have put on Gaza in the last year. This is key to bring a degree of stability. We need to work with Israel and the U.N. to finetune how we provide aid to Gaza. And, finally, we need to engage Arab countries, particularly those that have negative perceptions of Hamas, to get them to be more active. I am thinking United Arab Emirates, Saudi Arabia, working through Egypt.

Fourth, and quite importantly in my view, is the issue of Palestinian reform. This is an issue that has been on the back burner since the days of George W. Bush. This is key. When 80 percent of the Palestinians believe that their government is corrupt, it is very hard to see how they will trust this government to make the kind of concessions that need to be made.

In conclusion, I would say, none of the above will bring peace. Peace can only come in a two-state solution that is negotiated between the parties. What these measures, though, can do is that they can stabilize the situation on the ground, buy us time, and if the sides are wise and employ the right kind of political messaging, they can start reversing some of the negative perceptions that each side has of the other.

Thank you very much. And I am looking forward to the questions.

[The prepared statement of Mr. al-Omari follows:]

Israel, the Palestinians, and the Administration's Peace Plan

Ghaith al-Omari
Senior Fellow, Irwin Levy Family Program on the U.S.-Israel Strategic Relationship
The Washington Institute for Near East Policy

Testimony submitted to the Subcommittee on the Middle East and North Africa
February 14, 2018

Chairman Ros-Lehtinen, Ranking Member Deutch, and members of the subcommittee, thank you for the opportunity to appear before you to discuss Israel, the Palestinians and the Administration's peace plan. My testimony will examine the regional implications of recent developments in the peace process, particularly as they relate to the Palestinian Authority and Arab states. It will further look into a potential peace plan by the Administration and will conclude with recommendations for practical steps to advance the peace process.

INTRODUCTION

In recent weeks, the Middle East peace process has witnessed a number of rapid developments. Yet in the absence of a framework and sense of direction, much of this energy has been wasted or even negative. Without a clear articulation by the administration of a direction and a diplomatic strategy, the current state of drift is likely to continue and worsen. Nonetheless, as the administration formulates a plan, it needs to be careful not to overreach. Current political realities in both the Palestinian Authority (PA) and Israel make it difficult to envisage a peace plan that will meet the minimum needed substantively and politically by both parties to reengage in negotiations. Given the volatility of the situation on the ground, presenting a plan with a high likelihood of failure could trigger sharp deterioration. Instead, the United States should develop more modest objectives for the immediate term and engage Arab and European partners to build a wide U.S.-led coalition capable of navigating the current crisis. Most important, the United States can support security, economic, and governance improvements on the ground that will create conditions conducive to the resumption of meaningful negotiations.

BACKGROUND

The peace process has been officially suspended since 2014, but even before that—and despite intensive efforts by former secretary of state John Kerry—it was clear that the negotiations were heading to fail-

33

ure. Since coming to office, President Donald J. Trump has signaled his intent to pursue a resolution of the Palestinian-Israeli conflict. Trump entrusted his senior advisor Jared Kushner to oversee the effort and appointed longtime associates as well as established foreign policy professionals to oversee the process. On the diplomatic front, Israeli prime minister Benjamin Netanyahu and Palestinian president Mahmoud Abbas, as well as key regional leaders, were received in the White House, and Trump, in turn, visited Israel and the PA. Substantively, the U.S. peace team remained largely in "listening mode" during the first year, conducting wide-ranging meetings but giving no hint as to the administration's policies and strategy beyond its intention to present a plan at some point.[1]

THE JERUSALEM DECISION

This quiet diplomacy changed on December 6. Delivering on a campaign promise, Trump recognized Jerusalem as Israel's capital.[2] This action was undeniably within the sovereign right of the United States; furthermore, there had been no question throughout all past negotiations that in any final peace agreement West Jerusalem, as well as mutually-agreed parts of East Jerusalem, would be under Israeli sovereignty. Given Jerusalem's sensitivity, however, the PA and Arab states were bound to react negatively.

Had the decision been coordinated with Arab allies, some of their concerns could have been reflected in the framing of the decision, which would have provided them with some political breathing space vis-à-vis those seeking to further inflame emotions. Moreover, conflicting messages from the administration further complicated efforts to manage diplomatic fallout in the region. Trump's December 6 speech stated explicitly that the United States is "not taking a position [on] any final status issues, including the specific boundaries of the Israeli sovereignty in Jerusalem, or the resolution of contested borders." Yet the administration's public messaging, did not highlight this, and Trump's subsequent statements that he "took Jerusalem off the table" made it difficult for moderate voices to argue that the decision did not prejudge final peace talks.[3]

Predictably, the Palestinian leadership vehemently opposed the decision. A combination of Jerusalem's centrality to the Palestinian narrative and its diplomatic position, as well as the political weakness of President Abbas—with current approval ratings of only 31% among his public[4]—meant that Abbas felt—as a matter of both principle and political calculation—that he had to take hardline positions lest Fatah rivals and Hamas foes accuse him of abandoning Jerusalem. Abbas issued harsh statements that in some instances crossed into the unacceptable territory of denying Jewish connection to the land.[5] The United States should continue to insist that Abbas retract such statements.

Diplomatically, the PA suspended contact with the United States on peace-process-related matters, and resorted to the UN, eliciting a U.S. veto in the Security Council but securing a General Assembly resolution critical of the U.S. decision. Furthermore, the PLO made a number of decisions calling for severing relations—including security cooperation—with Israel and abandoning the Oslo Accords framework.[6] It should be noted, though, that similar decisions made in the past were not implemented. While the PA is likely to continue its internationalization campaign, security cooperation with Israel continues.

Arab states were bound to be critical of the decision both out of genuine disagreement with its substance and for political reasons. Jordan, with its longstanding special role as custodian of Muslim holy sites in Jerusalem—a role recognized by Israel in the two countries' 1994 peace treaty[7]—was particularly affected by the decision. Yet some moderate Arab states—particularly Jordan, Saudi Arabia, Egypt, and the

United Arab Emirates (UAE)—are trying to ensure that this does not develop into a full-blown crisis. These states are now seeking to isolate the issue of Jerusalem from their bilateral relations with the United States[8] while emphasizing that U.S. leadership of the peace process is indispensable.[9][10]

These efforts, however, are complicated by other regional actors who are using the decision to score political points. Iran and Qatar—in the context of their ongoing tensions with moderate Arab states—tried to cast the latter as complicit in the decision,[11][12] while Turkey president Recep Tayyip Erdogan is capitalizing on angry public sentiment to position himself as leader of the Muslim world.[13] Moreover, this decision has weakened the leverage of the moderate Arab states vis-à-vis the PA. While some of these states have privately urged the Palestinians to tone down their reaction, they feel they have to be careful in public for fear of being accused of abandoning Jerusalem and the Palestinian issue.

Washington can support moderate Arab states by highlighting that the Jerusalem decision does not prejudice the outcome of negotiations. The president[14] and administration[15] have recently begun to do so, but only a more robust outreach to Arab media will convey this message to Arab audiences.

PRESSURING THE PA

The Palestinian statements and actions following the Jerusalem decision elicited strong U.S. reactions, including threats of cutting off aid to pressure the PA, particularly regarding the United Nations Relief and Works Agency (UNRWA). On January 2, U.S. ambassador to the United Nations Nikki Haley indicated that Washington will cut aid to UNRWA "until the Palestinians agree to come to the table,"[16] and on January 16 the United States withheld $65 million of the $120 million installment for "future consideration."[17] President Trump also indicated that the administration may cut other forms of aid to apply pressure on the PA,[18] although it is not yet clear yet what this will mean.

Without question, UNRWA needs significant reform—a point recognized by the organization itself.[19] Furthermore, it is not appropriate that the United States bear a disproportionate share of financial support to the organization. Indeed, the decision to withhold a portion of the U.S. funding has already prompted international actors to take action. For example, Jordan's foreign minister recently called on Arab states to "shoulder our responsibilities" in supporting UNRWA.[20] Moreover, using aid to pressure the PA is a legitimate tool that could, if deployed properly, be effective in changing PA behavior.

In reality, however, these attempts to pressure the PA have so far not been effective. Fundamentally, it is not clear to what end U.S. pressure is being applied. Although the president and administration urge the PA to "come to the table" and "negotiate peace," there are, at this point, no negotiations, nor is there, at least for now, a concrete U.S. proposal to restart them. Therefore the PA has been able to cast this pressure in a punitive light.

Furthermore, the lack of coordination between the United States and key international actors has allowed the PA to evade pressure. In the past, leverage on the PA was successful when a coalition of relevant allies shared U.S. objectives, a reality vividly demonstrated during the George W. Bush administration. The PA realized it has no choice but to engage in reform or face regional and global isolation only when the U.S. message was amplified by European and Arab allies who refused to break ranks with Washington.

More specifically, defunding UNRWA—apart from its humanitarian implications—is unlikely to make a difference to the PA. Public discontent over cuts in UNRWA services will likely be directed, not against the PA, but against the United States, Israel, and UNRWA itself—and the PA can side with its public in expressing outrage. Furthermore, the PA is aware that Israel[21] also does not want to see deterioration in the West Bank and will likely, along with Arab states, lobby the United States against immediate cuts of UNRWA aid.

Instead, any significant reduction of UNRWA aid would most seriously harm Jordan, where UNRWA provides services to more than 2 million registered refugees, including 120,000 students and health facilities that processed 1.5 million patient visits in 2016. Transferring these responsibilities to Jordan will put pressure on an already strained infrastructure. But the concern is not only economic. Since the Arab protests in 2011, refugee camps in Jordan have remained quiet, including during the current wave of protests against the recent lifting of subsidies. Cutting UNRWA services will likely cause protests in Palestinian refugee camps.

AN AMERICAN PEACE PLAN?

The administration has repeatedly stated that it is working on a peace plan to be unveiled at some point in the future. Although, a U.S.-brokered plan to prompt negotiations and bridge differences ultimately has value, in practice, any plan presented in the short term is likely to fail due to the domestic politics of both Israel and the PA. Prime minister Netanyahu presides over a coalition that gives him an extremely narrow margin in which to maneuver. Members of his coalition who have been unwilling to allow for even the limited steps recommended by the Israel Defense Forces to alleviate the humanitarian situation in the West Bank[22] are unlikely to be willing to endorse the "hard compromises for peace"[23] envisioned by President Trump.

On the Palestinian side, Abbas's margin for maneuvering is also extremely limited. Failure of the peace process, corruption, and poor governance combined have severely eroded the PA's legitimacy among its public. Recent polls show that 77% of Palestinians believe that the PA is corrupt,[24] and 70% want Abbas to resign.[25] Add to that the split between the West Bank and Gaza, and the hardening of positions in the wake of the Jerusalem decision, then Abbas currently lacks the political credit needed to be able to engage with a peace plan that requires significant compromise.

Arab states, whose participation will be key, may be able to privately pressure Abbas to engage an American peace plan if its terms are reasonable. But even at the best of times, Arab leaders have been reluctant to break ranks with the PA in public, and this is further exacerbated by the negative public mood in the region following the Jerusalem decision.

A failed peace plan that is rejected by one or both parties will be costly. Among both the Palestinian and Israeli public, belief in peace is eroding[26] and another failed peace initiative will only solidify such skepticism. Among the Palestinians, given the tension and volatility on the ground and the weakness of the PA, another failed peace initiative could lead to an array of concrete negative results ranging from a sharp deterioration in the security situation to a potential collapse of the PA. Needless to say, severe disruption on the ground is not in the interest of the Palestinians, Israel, the region, or the United States.

RECOMMENDATIONS

While a full-fledged American peace plan may be premature, neglect is equally counterproductive. It may be more feasible at the moment to focus instead on less ambitious but more achievable goals that can stabilize the diplomatic scene and the situation on the ground. This would eventually create conditions conducive to the resumption of meaningful negotiations.

Diplomatic Steps

The diplomatic priority now is to break the current escalatory dynamic and provide a U.S.-led framework within which all parties, including the PA, can resume dialogue. A multilateral approach can provide an effective vehicle to that end. For example, despite the PA's decision to not engage the United States, Palestinian officials participated in a recent meeting of the Ad Hoc Liaison Committee (AHLC)—the international grouping dealing with economic and humanitarian aid to the PA—alongside the United States, Israel, Arab States and other international donors.[27]

Building on that precedent, the International Quartet (composed of the United States, the UN, the European Union, and Russia) should be reenergized to provide an umbrella under which the PA can reengage in U.S.-led peace diplomacy. Expanding the Quartet to include Jordan and Egypt would give it a regional dimension, and including Norway, which chairs the AHLC, would help better integrate political and economic issues.

Practical Steps

Important as diplomacy is, it is by nature slow-acting and ill-suited for responding to concrete, immediate developments on the ground, particularly as these realities remain prone to rapid deterioration. Therefore, as Washington continues to explore diplomatic options, administration attention in the immediate term should be turned toward creating practical, positive developments on the ground. While such developments are no replacement for diplomatic negotiations, positive developments on the ground will help stabilization and can start addressing each public's mistrust and negative view of the other.

In that regard, the United States should focus on the following areas:

1. SECURITY: Security is the sine qua non for any diplomatic, economic, or governance progress. Over the last decade, the security situation in the West Bank remained manageable, due to no small part to actions of the PA security forces (PASF), and their cooperation with their Israeli counterparts. The United States, through the U.S. Security Coordinator (USSC) for Israel and the Palestinian Authority, has been instrumental in reforming and professionalizing the PASF, and in shepherding security cooperation. The United States should continue to focus on the primacy of security and help support this virtuous dynamic.

   Specifically, the United States should continue directly supporting the PASF, maintain and strengthen the USSC, and engage Israel on ways to allow the continued growth of the PASF without endangering Israel's security, including increasing the PASF's jurisdiction to additional West

Bank areas. Finally, the United States, directly and through allies, should impress upon the PA the need to stop threatening to sever security cooperation, as such threats—even if not intended for implementation—delegitimize the PASF and demoralize its members.

2. GAZA: The situation in Gaza is fast approaching a humanitarian crisis.[28] Apart from its obvious and catastrophic human implications, such deterioration could lead to a new war. Ideally, assistance to Gaza should be channeled through the PA, to avoid Hamas benefiting from such aid. However, the recent Egyptian-led "reconciliation" talks—or, more accurately, talks aimed at reintroducing the PA into Gaza—have faltered. This was due to a large extent to the PA's unwillingness to assume authority over Gaza as long as Hamas continued to refuse to disarm. At the moment, Egypt, due to internal developments, is not actively pursuing Palestinian reconciliation talks. When Egypt reengages, however, the United States should continue to support its efforts to create—at a minimum—a measure of PA presence in Gaza to facilitate international aid.

That point, however, seems distant at the moment. In the immediate term, the United States should focus specifically on the following:

- pressuring Abbas—directly and through allies—to reverse his recent sanctions against the coastal Strip, including limiting electricity supply and other forms of payments to Gaza;[29]

- continuing to work with Israel and the U.N. to fine-tune existing mechanisms for humanitarian aid delivery; and

- engaging Egypt and Arab states to increase support to Gaza that bypasses Hamas' government.

3. THE WEST BANK: While Gaza's immediate concerns need to be addressed, the West Bank should not be taken for granted. The continuation of the Israeli occupation, the increased disbelief in the possibility of diplomatic progress, and eroding legitimacy of the PA due in part to poor governance and political stagnation has created an increasingly tense situation. Recent development regarding Jerusalem have further increased the tension. Yet due to the relative stability and the effective Palestinian-Israeli security cooperation, the Israeli defense establishment is supportive of a number measures to ease life on the ground. Some of these projects, however, fell victim to maneuverings among Israeli politicians[30].

The United States should urge Israel to implement—and to the extent possible avoid politicizing—such IDF-approved measures, specifically those which provide the Palestinians with economic access to Area "C" of the West Bank and grant the PA additional planning and zoning powers around congested Palestinian urban areas.

4. PALESTINIAN REFORM: Finally, the United States should refocus on promoting Palestinian reform. Besides the desirability, in its own right, of creating clean, effective governance in the PA, the widespread perception of corruption in the PA and general dissatisfaction with its performance has implications for the peace process. It erodes the legitimacy of Palestinian leaders, reducing their ability to reengage in negotiations, let alone make the necessary compromises for peace. As demonstrated under President George W. Bush, sustained U.S. prioritization of Palestinian reform can

produce dramatic results that increase the PA's legitimacy among its public and Israel's trust of the PA as a peace partner.

In addition to direct U.S. engagement on the issue, the administration should explore a role for Arab states in Palestinian reform, especially roles in which some—like the UAE and Jordan—have developed significant capacity as they undertook their own processes of reform and institution building.

---

[1] http://www.jpost.com/International/Liberman-Trump-administration-still-in-listening-and-learning-mode-497453

[2] https://www.whitehouse.gov/briefings-statements/statement-president-trump-jerusalem/

[3] https://www.whitehouse.gov/briefings-statements/remarks-president-trump-prime-minister-netanyahu-israel-bilateral-meeting-davos-switzerland/

[4] http://www.pcpsr.org/sites/default/files/poll%2066%20full%20text%20English%20Dec%202017.pdf

[5] https://www.timesofisrael.com/rewriting-history-abbas-calls-israel-a-colonial-project-unrelated-to-judaism/

[6] http://www.jpost.com/Arab-Israeli-Conflict/Palestinian-Central-Council-calls-upon-PLO-to-end-recognition-of-Israel-536845

[7] http://www.mfa.gov.il/mfa/foreignpolicy/peace/guide/pages/israel-jordan%20peace%20treaty.aspx

[8] https://www.reuters.com/article/us-usa-israel-pence-jordan/pence-says-he-and-jordans-king-abdullah-agreed-to-disagree-on-jerusalem-idUSKBN1FA0V5

[9] https://in.reuters.com/article/usa-trump-saudi/u-s-mideast-peace-plan-not-finalised-but-efforts-serious-says-saudis-jubeir-idINKBN1E81PX

[10] https://www.politico.com/story/2018/02/04/jordan-abdullah-jerusalem-israel-389573

[11] http://washin.st/2CfSliA (Arabic)

[12] http://washin.st/2o233tB (Arabic)

[13] https://www.alaraby.co.uk/english/news/2017/12/13/erdogan-seeks-to-unite-muslim-leaders-over-jerusalem

[14] http://www.israelhayom.com/2018/02/11/trump-to-israel-hayom-palestinians-are-not-looking-to-make-peace/

[15] https://useu.usmission.gov/remarks-ad-hoc-liaison-committee-meeting/

[16] https://www.timesofisrael.com/us-warns-it-wont-fund-refugee-agency-if-palestinians-reject-talks/

[17] https://www.npr.org/sections/thetwo-way/2018/01/17/578571424/u-s-freezes-more-than-half-of-aid-to-u-n-agency-for-palestinian-refugees

[18] https://www.whitehouse.gov/briefings-statements/remarks-president-trump-prime-minister-netanyahu-israel-bilateral-meeting-davos-switzerland/

[19] https://www.unrwa.org/who-we-are/reforming-unrwa

[20] https://twitter.com/AymanHsafadi/status/959800386285600768

[21] http://www.jpost.com/Arab-Israeli-Conflict/Trump-cuts-UNRWA-funding-amid-Abbas-assault-536917

[22] https://www.timesofisrael.com/cabinet-puts-temporary-freeze-on-qalqilya-expansion-plan/

[23] https://www.timesofisrael.com/trump-tells-israel-it-will-have-to-make-hard-compromises-for-peace/

[24] http://www.pcpsr.org/en/node/715

[25] http://www.pcpsr.org/en/node/715

[26] http://www.pcpsr.org/en/node/717

[27] https://www.norway.no/en/indonesia/norway-indonesia/news-events/news2/extraordinary-meeting-of-the-international-donor-group-for-palestine-ahlc-in-brussels/

[28] https://www.timesofisrael.com/idf-chief-said-to-warn-gaza-war-likely-if-humanitarian-crisis-persists/

[29] http://www.dailystar.com.lb/News/Middle-East/2017/Aug-07/415205-abbas-pledges-to-ramp-up-gaza-strip-sanctions.ashx

[30] https://www.timesofisrael.com/cabinet-puts-temporary-freeze-on-qalqilya-expansion-plan/

Ms. Ros-Lehtinen. Thank you very much. You must be a favorite on the speaking circuit, because you are brief, to the point, and boom, boom, boom. Thank you so much.

Mr. al-Omari. That is my legal education.

Ms. Ros-Lehtinen. That is your schtick. All right, thank you.

Ambassador Shapiro, welcome, and thank you so much for being with us.

STATEMENT OF THE HONORABLE DANIEL B. SHAPIRO, DISTINGUISHED VISITING FELLOW, INSTITUTE FOR NATIONAL SECURITY STUDIES (FORMER UNITED STATES AMBASSADOR TO ISRAEL)

Mr. Shapiro. Madam Chairman, Ranking Member Deutch, it is good to see you both. Members of the committee, thank you for the opportunity to testify today on a subject that is really what motivated me to get involved in public life and, indeed, brought me to my first job, on the staff of this very committee, 25 years ago.

It was my judgment then and remains my judgment now that the two-state solution is the only outcome that can serve Israel's interests in security, recognition, and maintaining its Jewish and democratic character, Palestinian legitimate aspirations for self-determination and an independent state of their own at peace with Israel, and American interests in ensuring those outcomes and contributing to regional stability.

Now, despite many predictions to the contrary, for the most part, the Trump administration has pursued an approach, if not a defined policy, well within the mainstream of traditional U.S. policy on this issue. While the President does not speak clearly in support of a two-state solution as the goal of U.S. policy, as I believe he should, his description of what he wants included in the "ultimate deal" leaves no doubt that there is no other outcome that would achieve all of those objectives.

Other familiar elements of the policy include positive meetings with leaders of both sides, envoys who have earned goodwill and credibility throughout the region, a commitment to Palestinian economic development, and a clear, if somewhat more muted, effort to restrain Israel settlement construction.

I agree, as has been stated, that there has been a lack of clarity, and it has been compounded by some of the President's confusing tweets. But I have to say that, while I have had many, many profound disagreements with the Trump administration on a wide range of issues, the issue that concerns me the least is their efforts to advance Israeli-Palestinian peace.

But they have missed important opportunities and hit some bumps. The poor management of the decision regarding Jerusalem made things harder. Now, I strongly support recognition of Jerusalem as Israel's capital and the immediate relocation of our Embassy there. But had the decision been described in the broader context of the U.S. vision of a two-state solution, including addressing Palestinian aspirations in East Jerusalem, it would have both acknowledged an obvious fact and helped advance our strategic objective.

None of that justifies the Palestinian overreaction, including the outrageous speech President Abbas delivered to the PLO's Central

Council that has already been referenced. In my judgment, in that speech, President Abbas signaled the end of his own personal participation in efforts to achieve the two-state solution.

This chain of events has left the Trump administration in a bind, with no way to get their plan out, at least until tempers cool somewhat, without it being dead on arrival.

But, in fairness, there is currently no chance for an immediate breakthrough toward a peace agreement or even the resumption of negotiations. That is partially due to domestic political crises on both sides that have been referenced, partly due to the deep mutual mistrust, the waves of Palestinian terrorist attacks, the continued incitement and glorification of violence by Palestinian leaders, and Hamas' continued construction of rockets and tunnels. Those are all factors. So is the timidity of Arab states in beginning normalization with Israel. So is the Israeli settlement expansion, including in areas well beyond the settlement blocs near the 1967 lines, which makes a viable map of the two-state solution more difficult over time.

In addition to Abbas' negative turn, it should also be recognized that the current Israeli Government is dominated by voices who openly oppose a two-state solution. That poses a major challenge to Prime Minister Netanyahu, who, while he is more ambiguous than he was in the past, has not walked back his famous 2009 Bar-Ilan University speech endorsing two states.

So, in the current circumstances, I do not recommend that the administration try to bring the parties back to the negotiating table in the near future. Any talks they could arrange would almost certainly collapse, perhaps spectacularly.

Rather, the administration should focus on preserving the two-state solution as a viable and achievable goal for the future, but postponing any actual negotiations until the atmosphere and the leadership dynamics have improved, almost certainly including new Palestinian leadership.

First, keeping the two-state solution alive requires clarity from the United States that that is the outcome that remains our strategic objective.

Then we should work with all relevant parties to take practical steps that put down anchors to help arrest the slide toward a binational reality: For Israel, expanding the areas in which Palestinian Authority can operate, permitting greater Palestinian economic development, and limiting construction in West Bank settlements to areas that can be accommodated in equivalent land swaps in a final status agreement.

For Palestinians, continuing and upgrading their effective security cooperation with Israel and conducting a consistent campaign against incitement of violence and glorification of those who commit acts of terror. The Taylor Force Act will hopefully hasten the end of those unacceptable payments.

For Arab states who already see Israel as a strategic partner against common enemies, beginning now to engage Israel in steps toward normalization.

Finally, I hope the committee will support continuing those elements of our Palestinian assistance program that support security cooperation between Israel and the P.A. And contribute to improving humanitarian conditions for the Palestinian people. Congress should also consider additional approaches such as broader support for people-to-people programs and investing in the Palestinian high-tech sector.

But looking a bit beyond the immediate policy questions, no matter how much Congress or the administration do, we should recognize that trends on the ground pose the danger of an unarrested drift toward a binational state. Many younger Palestinians say they are no longer focused on the goal of a two-state solution. Rather, they advocate holding out for full equal rights, with one person, one vote, in a single state. We should hear those voices.

I also listen closely to the views of many of the ministers in the current Israeli Government, people with whom I have worked and consider friends even when we disagree, who oppose a two-state solution. They are very open about it and very sincere in favoring other options. I believe these options actually deserve greater study, because we might end up in one of them.

But all of them are worse than a two-state solution. All of them would pose challenge to Israel's status as a Jewish and democratic state and its ability to maintain its security. Any could lead to renewed and sustained conflict. None deliver on Palestinians' legitimate aspirations for independence. And they would squander the real opportunity that exists for normalization between Israel and the Arab states. For all of those reasons, they would be worse from the point of view of U.S. interests.

I worry about the implications of those outcomes for the bilateral U.S.-Israel relationship as well, which is both a strategic asset and a moral obligation. I have spent virtually my entire life working to build, support, and strengthen that relationship, including in the negotiations to produce the $38 billion memorandum of understanding. I agree with former Vice President Biden, who said, "If Israel did not exist, we would have to invent it" because of the benefit this partnership provides for U.S. interests.

So if we find ourselves drifting toward some version of the binational state, we should study carefully what would be the impacts on our relationship. If we go down that road, I favor doing it with our eyes open, as allies, trying to steer toward the least bad outcome.

Thank you again for the opportunity to address the committee, and I look forward to answering any questions.

[The prepared statement of Mr. Shapiro follows:]

Testimony of Daniel B. Shapiro
Distinguished Visiting Fellow, Institute for National Security Studies, Tel Aviv
House Committee on Foreign Affairs, Subcommittee on the Middle East and North
Africa
"Israel, the Palestinians, and the Administration's Peace Plan"
February 14, 2018

Madam Chairman, Ranking Member Deutch, Members of the Committee, thank you for
the opportunity to testify today on current developments in the Israeli-Palestinian arena,
prospects for renewed negotiations, and the Trump Administration's efforts and policies
on this issue.

I should note at the outset that I remain an unabashed promoter and supporter of a two-
state solution as the only solution to the Israeli-Palestinian conflict. That is the issue that
motivated me to get involved in public life, and indeed, brought me to my first
government job on the staff of this Committee under its then-Chairman, Lee Hamilton,
just after the signing of the Oslo Accords nearly 25 years ago. I hoped then, and I
continue to hope today, that I could make some small contribution to achieving this
elusive but important goal.

It was my judgment then and throughout a career of increasingly intensive involvement
in these negotiations that the two-state solution is the only outcome that can serve Israel's
interests in security, recognition, and maintaining its Jewish and democratic character;
Palestinian legitimate aspirations for self-determination in an independent state of their
own at peace with Israel; and American interests in ensuring those outcomes and
contributing to regional stability. For all the difficulties, that remains my judgment
today.

The current outlook is quite bleak. Two weeks ago, at the annual conference of the
Institute for National Security Studies in Tel Aviv, where I am a visiting fellow, the
Trump Administration's special envoy expressed some frustration with the current
stalemate. It was impossible for me not to feel sympathy. I've been there. A long line of
American negotiators, with goodwill, good ideas, and good intentions, have run aground
on the shoals of Israelis' and Palestinians' mistrust of one another, waves of Palestinian
terror, paralyzing domestic politics, timidity on the part of Arab states, and Israeli
settlement expansion. So the current sense of a diplomatic effort with no realistic
prospect of a breakthrough is depressingly familiar.

Following our presidential election and during my final months serving as Ambassador, I
heard many predictions that President-elect Trump would end US advocacy for a two-
state solution, lend support to Israeli annexation of some or all of the West Bank, cut off

relations with the Palestinian Authority, and end U.S. opposition to Israeli settlement construction.

None of those have turned out to be the case. Throughout most of 2017, the Administration pursued an approach that was well within the mainstream of traditional U.S. policy. The President hosted Israeli Prime Minister Netanyahu and Palestinian Authority President Mahmoud Abbas in a warm, productive atmosphere. He made a successful visit to the region in May, convincing leaders on all sides of his desire to achieve a peace agreement. His envoys, Jason Greenblatt and Jared Kushner, traveled the region and built up considerable goodwill and a positive impression of their empathy, creativity, and realism about what a peace agreement required. Parties throughout the region and elsewhere waited expectantly for the President to publish his plan. Had he done so at a couple of key junctures in 2017, when his leverage was at its highest, he would have been very hard to say no to.

True, the President avoided a clear commitment to a two-state solution, talking of "the ultimate deal" and saying first that he would support whatever the parties could agree to, and then making clear that the options for the parties' agreement included a two-state solution. But despite that lack of clarity — a mistake, in my view — he nevertheless described his aspiration to achieve a peace agreement, reached in direct negotiations between Israelis and Palestinians, that delivered security for Israelis, provided self-determination for Palestinians, and would enable the opening of Israel's relations with much of the Arab world. With three decades of experience in the region behind me, I feel confident in saying that there is no outcome other than a two-state solution that would achieve all those objectives.

Other familiar elements of the policy included an oft-stated commitment to Palestinian economic development, and a clear effort to restrain Israeli settlement construction. The latter effort was more muted than in the past, and perhaps more flexible, but there is no question that the expectations of some settlement advocates in Israel that a Trump Administration would herald the end of American concern about that issue, were not met — to the point that these advocates have complained vocally to Prime Minister Netanyahu about the lack of construction approvals. As recently as this week, in an interview with the Israeli newspaper *Israel HaYom*, the President said that settlements "complicated making peace", and that "Israel has to be very careful with the settlements".

Since the day he was inaugurated, I have had many profound disagreements with the Trump Administration on a wide range of issues. But through most of 2017, the issue that concerned me the least was their efforts to advance Israeli-Palestinian peace.

Having said that, they have hit several significant bumps recently, including through self-inflicted mistakes, that have set back much of what they achieved in the early months.

Most notable was the poor management of the decision regarding Jerusalem. Now, I want to be clear: I strongly support recognition of Jerusalem as Israel's capital, and the immediate relocation of our embassy there. Such recognition acknowledges an obvious fact, and one which we accept functionally in our work with the Israeli government in its offices in Jerusalem. It also helpfully punctures a myth too-often trafficked by Palestinians that there is no historic Jewish connection to Jerusalem, an element of the broader campaign of delegitimization of Israel's very existence.

On October 24, several weeks before the decision, I published in the *Wall Street Journal* an op-ed describing what I considered the smart way to do the right thing — namely, to recognize Jerusalem as Israel's capital and move the embassy to West Jerusalem, and simultaneously to describe those moves in the broader context of the U.S. vision of a two-state solution, including acknowledgment that East Jerusalem has a different status, must be negotiated, and must, in the end, include the capital of a Palestinian state in at least some of its Arab neighborhoods as part of a unified city.

At a minimum, it made little sense to make this announcement before the Kushner/Greenblatt plan had been presented, and without placing the Jerusalem issue in a broader context. Sequenced properly, recognition of Jerusalem as Israel's capital would have both righted a historic wrong *and* helped advance our strategic objective. The strategic objective is not where our embassy sits. It is the end of the Israeli-Palestinian conflict in a two-state solution with peace, security, and mutual recognition for both sides.

President Trump did none of those things. Evidently motivated by the deadline requiring him to issue another waiver of the Jerusalem Embassy Act of 1995, by all accounts he surprised his own staff and overrode the concerns of his cabinet secretaries in insisting on immediate recognition. A poorly prepared and clumsily rolled-out decision, without prior consultation with a range of key regional parties, compounded the problem. Even important caveats, clarifying that the borders of sovereignty in Jerusalem would need to be negotiated, were ignored in the shuffle, and then undermined by the President's imprecise comments that he had "taken Jerusalem off the table", before he got around to reiterating them in his *Israel HaYom* interview this week. The decision would never have been welcomed by the Palestinians, but the President did everything possible to make it difficult for them to absorb.

None of that justifies the Palestinian overreaction. On January 14, 2018, President Abbas delivered a truly outrageous speech to the PLO Central Council in which he bizarrely described Israel as the product of a European colonialist plot, repeated the canard that Israel has no organic connection to Jewish history, and shamefully accused Israel of importing drugs to poison Palestinian children. He also unrealistically demanded that the United States be replaced as the mediator of Middle East peace talks.

In my judgment, in this speech, President Abbas signaled the end of his personal participation in efforts to achieve a two-state solution. If, in earlier stages of his career, he was conflicted — both participating in negotiations toward that end and authorizing impressive security coordination with Israel, and finding it difficult to tell hard truths to his people about Israel's permanence and legitimacy and the unacceptability of terror — he now appears to have cast his lot. As the succession struggle for the Palestinian leadership following Abbas unfolds, he seems determined to end his career as one who refused to relinquish key Palestinian dogmas about Israel.

This chain of events has left the Trump Administration paralyzed. With Abbas high up in a tree, the Administration has made no effort to find a ladder to help him climb down. The President's tweets complaining about the Palestinians' refusal to negotiate — oddly out of sequence, in that he has still not presented his plan that was intended to be the basis for negotiations — and his threat to cut off U.S. assistance programs to the Palestinians, only sent Abbas higher.

So in the current circumstance, the Administration has no way to get their plan out, at least until tempers cool somewhat, without it being dead on arrival. I hope the Administration will resist the advice they are getting from some quarters to rush out a one-sided plan in full knowledge that the Palestinians will reject it out of hand. That would deal yet another blow to the already battered prospects for two states.

The truth is that a realistic assessment tells us that the current situation offers no chance for an immediate breakthrough toward a peace agreement, or even the resumption of negotiations. The weight of the failure of the negotiations of 2010 and 2013-14 remains heavy, deepening the near total mistrust that existed between Netanyahu and Abbas even before they started those talks. Several waves of Palestinian stabbing and car-ramming terrorist attacks, and Hamas' continued construction of rockets and tunnels to attack Israel have done much to engender doubts among Israelis that there is a viable partner for peace. So has the continued incitement and glorification of violence by Palestinians leaders, including the unconscionable salaries paid to Palestinian terrorists with blood on their hands in Israeli prisons. Israeli settlement expansion, including in areas well beyond the settlement blocs near the 1967 lines which could be accommodated in territorial swaps, continues to make a viable map of a two-state solution more difficult over time. And Arab states, even those who perceive a strategic alignment with Israel vis-a-vis the common threats of Iran and Sunni extremists, have been far too timid about signaling to Israelis and Palestinians about what a post-peace regional alignment could look like, including by beginning steps of normalization with Israel.

I have already spoken about the turn that Abbas has taken away from being a viable partner for two states. His own domestic weakness, including his perpetual competition for influence with Hamas, makes it unlikely that will change.

Prime Minister Netanyahu faces his own challenges, including a spate of corruption investigations which he has responded to politically by pulling in close with his right-wing base. Reports that the Prime Minister told his party members he has been discussing annexation of West Bank settlements with the Administration are the most recent evidence of this trend. Needless to say, unilateral Israeli annexation, even of areas Israel could reasonably be expected to keep in the land swaps envisioned in a two-state solution, especially if disconnected from other final status issues, would deepen the crisis we find ourselves in, and make even more distant the needed resumption of negotiations. So I was encouraged that the White House denied that any such conversations had taken place.

It also should be recognized, as the President suggested in his interview this week in *Israel HaYom*, that the current Israeli government is dominated by voices who openly oppose the two-state solution. Netanyahu, who endorsed that outcome in 2009, has more recently remained ambiguous about the end-state he seeks. But most members of his government are clear in their opposition.

I do not recommend that the Administration make any effort to try to bring the parties back to the negotiating table in the near future. These parties are so far apart, and their history with and attitudes about one another are so toxic, that, even if the Administration managed, somehow, to drag them back to the table, the talks would almost certainly collapse, perhaps spectacularly. And such a collapse could easily be punctuated by another round of violence.

Rather, the Administration should approach this challenge with a view toward preserving the two-state solution as a viable and achievable goal for the future, but postponing any actual negotiations until the atmosphere has improved and there are appropriate changes in the leadership dynamic — almost certainly new Palestinian leadership and at least a different Israeli coalition.

A strategy aimed at keeping the two-state solution alive would start with clarity from the United States that that outcome remains our strategic objective, the end state that would best serve U.S. interests. Then, it would work with all relevant parties to take practical steps that put down anchors to help arrest the slide toward a binational reality.

For Israel, those steps include expanding the areas in which the Palestinian Authority can operate, by creating contiguity between disconnected areas of PA control (Areas A and B), and permitting greater Palestinian economic development in portions of Area C that would likely become part of a Palestinian state in a final status agreement. Israel should also define a policy on West Bank settlements that freezes construction in areas east of the security barrier and limits it to those areas within settlement blocs that can be accommodated in equivalent land swaps in a final status agreement. The important thing is to demonstrate, in word and deed, and by clear expressions of intent about where Israel intends to remain present and not to remain, that a two-state solution, including a viable Palestinian state, remains a realistic goal, even if it cannot be achieved anytime soon, and even if it will require new Palestinian leaders to accept and teach their public about Israel's legitimacy and permanence in ways they have not done heretofore.

For Palestinians, preserving the possibility of a two-state solution means continuing, and upgrading, the effective security coordination the PA Security Forces have been engaged in with their Israeli counterparts, including expanding their presence to agreed parts of Area B. It also requires a consistent campaign against incitement to violence and glorification of those who commit acts of terror. These outrageous practices, which teach young Palestinians that violence against civilians is acceptable, must stop. The Taylor Force Act, which is advancing through Congress, will hopefully hasten the end of the unacceptable payments to terrorists with blood on their hands. One additional gesture Palestinians should take is to swear off efforts to gang up on Israel and isolate it in international forums.

Arab states can make a significant contribution toward preserving the viability of two-states by beginning to act now, not waiting for later, on the recognition of the alignment of their interests and Israel's. Israel is already a strategic partner, openly acknowledged, to Saudi Arabia, the United Arab Emirates, and other moderate Sunni states — in addition to its peace partners, Egypt and Jordan. Those states should begin now to engage Israel in steps toward normalization — official diplomatic visits and meetings; academic and cultural exchanges; opening economic and trade links; permitting the overflight of Israeli commercial aircraft; and so on. Those gestures now will send signals to the Arab and Israeli publics about the benefits that can fully blossom in the context of a two-state solution. They should also be accompanied by signals to the Palestinians setting realistic expectations about final status issues like refugees returning to a Palestinian state but not to Israel itself, and the need to recognize Israel as a Jewish state.

Finally, it is important in the same period to continue to seek to improve the economic and humanitarian circumstances of Palestinians in the West Bank and Gaza. Doing so serves both the need to relieve suffering and upgrade living standards, which contributes to stability, and helps to build the foundations of the economy of an independent Palestinian state. U.S. assistance contributes greatly to these efforts, with very little actually reaching the accounts of the Palestinian Authority. That is why the President's tweets made little sense. The consequences of cutting off U.S. assistance would be to harm vulnerable Palestinians, including many children, and to impose a greater economic and security burden on Israel, which would have to fill the gaps in funding and services and deal with the security fallout.

Thankfully, it appears Special Envoy Greenblatt understands those dynamics. His continued visits to aid projects, partnership with Israeli military leaders in charge of civil

and economic affairs, and, most recently, his presentation at the Ad-Hoc Liaison
Committee (AHLC) donors meeting in Brussels last month indicate that the U.S.
approach is not, in fact to cut off assistance, but rather to continue it and seek other
partners to increase their contributions. The Israeli minister representing the Government
of Israel at the meeting, Tzachi Hanegbi, was no less enthusiastic about the importance or
pressing forward with economic and infrastructure projects in the West Bank and Gaza to
improve the quality of life for Palestinians. And the attendance of Palestinian Authority
Prime Minister Rami Hamadallah indicates that the diplomatic stalemate need not
prevent cooperation on economic advancement.

Most worrisome is the situation in Gaza, where years of Hamas' mismanagement and
squandering of resources on rockets, tunnels, and fruitless wars with Israel, and
Palestinian Authority ambivalence about taking on the responsibilities of governance
where it would need to challenge Hamas militarily — has left the population in
significant distress, with crumbling electricity, water, and and wastewater treatment
infrastructure and massive unemployment. The imperative of addressing the urgent
situation in Gaza is about relieving significant human misery, heading off health and
sanitation crises that no know borders, and easing tensions that could become the spark
for the next war between Israel and Hamas.

**My recommendation to the Committee is ensure the continuation of those elements
of our Palestinian assistance program that support security cooperation between
Israel and the PA, and contribute to improving humanitarian conditions to the
Palestinian people.** Those programs can be accommodated within the bounds of the
emerging version of the Taylor Force Act. It is simply a fact that a cut-off of U.S.
economic assistance would make it much harder, politically, for Palestinian security
partners to continue accept our security assistance. The breakdown of those programs,
and a humanitarian crisis in Gaza, are the most likely near-term causes of another wave
of violence or round of conflict in Gaza, which both pose significant security risks for
Israel. That is why the IDF leadership is so clear on the importance of continuing those
programs.

**One more contribution Congress can make is to increase funding for creative
approaches to sustaining prospects for two-states outside of traditional assistance
programs.** We have seen the impact of **people-to-people programs,** like the
Congressionally-mandated Conflict Management and Mitigation (CMM) grants, which
support NGOs that build people-to-people ties between Israelis and Palestinians, and
between different groups within each society. These programs build grassroots support
for reconciliation and conflict resolution, and increase support for and belief in a two-
state solution among those who take part.

Another opportunity would be to invest in **the emerging Palestinian hi-tech sector,**
which would create high quality jobs and expand existing channels of Israeli-Palestinian

hi-tech private sector collaboration. I refer the Committee to the article, "Start-Up Palestine: How to Spark a West Bank Tech Boom" by Yadin Kaufmann in the July/August 2017 issue of *Foreign Affairs*, for details on a proposal to pair Palestinian start-ups with established U.S. partner companies and receive grants to support R&D costs, modeled on the successful U.S.-Israel Binational Industrial Research and Development Foundation.

Any reduction in Palestinian assistance programs could be directed toward these efforts, without putting any money in the hands of the Palestinian Authority, and helping sustain the viability of the two state solution.

But no matter how much Congress contributes, and no matter much the Administration urges all parties to take the steps that will keep the two-state solution viable for the future, we shouldn't deceive ourselves. The situation on the ground, the periodic waves of violence, the political incentives for the main actors, the continued expansion of settlements, and the hardening of attitudes all point in the other direction. The danger we face is an unarrested drift in the direction of what the Prime Minister has called — and says he does not want — a binational state: a situation in which similar-sized Jewish and Arab populations live between the Jordan River and the Mediterranean Sea in the framework of one state. Even if you exclude Gaza from that calculation, the numbers point in that direction.

Today, many younger Palestinians say they are no longer focused on the goal of a two-state solution; rather, they advocate holding out for fully equal rights, with one-person one-vote, in a single state. We need to hear their voices.

I also listen closely to the views of many of the ministers in the current Israel government — people I have worked with and consider friends, even when we disagree — who oppose a two-state solution. They are very open about it, and are very sincere. Whether motivated by the Jewish people's historic and religious ties to the West Bank, the security challenges of withdrawal from those areas, the lack of confidence in the Palestinian leadership that will follow, or the chaos of the region that surrounds Israel on every side, they do no believe two states is desirable or workable, and they are working to prevent it.

Because of the prominence of these views in the Israeli government and influential constituencies, I have undertaken to study some of the alternatives to a two-state solution that those who hold these views propose. They include proposals to: annex all of the West Bank or the 60 percent that comprises Area C; apply civilian Israeli law to West Bank settlements that currently answer to the Israeli military; provide local autonomy to most Palestinians under overall Israeli sovereignty and security control; provide all, some, or no Palestinians in the West Bank with Israeli citizenship and voting rights in national elections; or make West Bank Palestinians citizens of Jordan.

I believe these options deserve greater study because we might end up in one of them. Or, there might be a determination to just try to muddle through with the status quo, which, of course, is not static. But all of these options are worse than a two-state solution. All of them would pose challenges to Israel's status as a Jewish and democratic state, and its ability to sustain its security. Many of them could lead to renewed and sustained conflict in a virtual civil war scenario. None of them deliver on Palestinians' legitimate aspirations for independence in a state that is at peace with Israel. They would very likely squander the real opportunity that exists today for normalization between Israel and Arab states, busting the irrational exuberance of some who believe the Arab states will normalize with Israel without regard to a stalemate on the Palestinian issue. And all of them would be worse from the point of view of U.S. interests.

I am particularly worried about the implications of these outcomes for the bilateral U.S.-Israel relationship. I have spent virtually my entire life trying to build, support, and strengthen that relationship, which encompasses extensive security coordination, the common values of two democracies, and a burgeoning economic partnership. I am proud of the extraordinary commitment of the United States to Israel's security — both a strategic asset and a moral obligation — which I was privileged to help advance in the negotiations that produced the $38 billion Memorandum of Understanding for the next decade of U.S. military assistance. I am in the school of former Vice President Joe Biden, who has said that if Israel did not exist, we would have to invent it, because of the benefit this partnership provides for U.S. interests.

But if we find ourselves drifting toward some version of the binational state, we should study carefully what would be the impacts on our relationship. Advocates for the alternatives should be asked to explain their perspective, being clear and honest about the impact of what they propose. My own worry is that if, over time, many in the world, quite a few Americans, and not a small number of Israelis raise questions about whether Israel continues to be the Jewish and democratic state it has always been and which is the fulfillment of the Zionist vision, when at least one of those aspects of its identity is under stress, it will put pressures on our bilateral relationship, which will begin to change in ways that are hard to predict. If we go down this road, I favor doing it with our eyes open, trying, as allies, to steer toward the least bad outcome.

Madam Chairman, Ranking Member Deutch, thank you again for the opportunity to address the Committee. I look forward to answering any questions.

Ms. Ros-Lehtinen. Thank you so much, Mr. Ambassador.

And we are thrilled with all of your testimonies.

And we will begin our question-and-answer period with Mr. DeSantis of Florida.

Mr. DeSantis. Thank you, Madam Chairman.

Mr. May, in the lead-up to the President's announcement of recognizing Jerusalem as Israel's capital, there were a lot of people saying that this would just light the world on fire, everything was going to end. He made the announcement. Obviously, there were some people that weren't happy, but we did not see the reaction that many people predicted. Is that correct?

Mr. May. Yes, that is correct. It was nothing like the predictions. There were announced 3 days of rage in the West Bank, but it was all fairly muted.

I think what is very important to recognize is, first of all, this is a recognition of reality. Second, this is a recognition of Israeli sovereignty. And it is very important to push back against the narrative produced by U.N. Security Council Resolution 2334 that you will hear, that Israel has no rights to be in Jerusalem whatsoever. It is important to disabuse Palestinians of the notion that the Jews will eventually be driven from Jerusalem, that eventually the Jewish state will be wiped out. If there is to be a Palestinian state, it must coexist peacefully with the Jewish state and recognize that.

And there hasn't been that recognition on the part, certainly, of Hamas, but also Mahmoud Abbas has not. And he has, in his most recent tirade, made very clear that he does not recognize the rights of a Jewish state to exist.

So this was an important bit of honesty. We should have recognition that Jerusalem will continue to be the capital before the peace process begins, not at the end. And the peace process should include a process of normalization of relations. We can't wait until the diplomats have shaken hands. The Palestinian people must learn that they are going to live with Israel, not wipe Israel off the map.

Mr. DeSantis. Yeah. I mean, I think you are right. I mean, this is a recognition of reality. And, first of all, the Jordanians, when they occupied it, that was not a legitimate sovereignty, after 1948. And I think only two countries recognized Jordanian sovereignty over Jerusalem and over the West Bank.

And I think one thing that we have seen since 1967, Jerusalem is really a jewel of the world. All faiths can go and pray and worship in the old city. That was not the case when the Arabs occupied Jerusalem. Jews were systematically excluded. Christians were treated as second-class citizens. And so Israeli sovereignty, they have a good track record, and the stewardship has been great.

In terms of moving forward, Mr. May, what has changed—has anything changed in Palestinian Arab society in terms of their views of the legitimacy of a Jewish state, in terms of their views of the Israelis?

I look at the textbooks in these schools. I look at them naming streets after terrorists. I look at the payments to the families of terrorists. And that seems to me to be something that is widely embraced by the Palestinian Arab society.

What are your thoughts on that?

Mr. MAY. You are exactly right, Congressman. There has been nothing productive that has taken place. It has gone in the wrong direction, I would say. We do not have Palestinian leaders attempting to prepare their people for the idea of peaceful coexistence. The anti-normalization campaign makes this very difficult.

In my testimony, I talk about SodaStream, Daniel Birnbaum. All he wanted to do was employ Palestinians and Israelis and Israeli Arabs, men and women, together in one place. And he found that he could do that, produce a good product, give good salaries. The BDS movement, or campaign, which is really what it is, was one of the reasons that factory, which was paying salaries four times what Palestinians could get elsewhere, was eventually shut down. If there is to be a peace process, it needs to start with the idea that we are going to develop neighborly and normal relations. And we don't have that at this moment. We don't have Palestinian lead- ers who are trying to prepare their people for peace. We have the celebration and incitement of terrorism and the rewarding of ter- rorists, that needs to change. And only then can a productive and realistic peace process, one that doesn't fail, as previous peace proc- esses have, only then can it begin.

Mr. DESANTIS. Ambassador Shapiro, you alluded to Netanyahu's support for a two-state solution. But if you listen to what he says, I mean, he does say that, but he wants, really, a neutered—something less than a state, it seems to me. Israel would still control the Jordan Valley. It would be a demilitarized state. So there would be perhaps some sovereignty, but they would not be permitted to exercise the full range of sovereignty.

Is that a fair reading of what Netanyahu has proposed? And what do you think of that vis-a-vis a full sovereignty?

Mr. SHAPIRO. I think his more recent statements have tended in the direction you are describing. He has sometimes used the phrase, "state minus." He has been more specific about the presence of the IDF after the end of that process than he had been previously. He has been clear that he doesn't envision the removal of Israeli settlements from any part of the West Bank, and definitely something far less than a fully sovereign state.

In his earlier statements, going back to the Bar-Ilan University speech, he was less specific and spoke about a demilitarized Palestinian state that recognizes the Jewish state. Perfectly reasonable and understandable conditions for the establishment of that state.

And I think everyone understands that the emergence of a Palestinian state after full recognition and with the full commitment to Israel's security needs will be sovereignty compromised to some degree, and its leaders would have to agree to that as part of the agreements and treaties establishing that state.

But there is probably a limit to what a Palestinian leader can sell to their own people as the achievement of Palestinian aspirations. And how it is described and what the specific functional aspects of those sovereignty limitations that are voluntary, that maybe include outsiders to help meet the security needs of all sides, is something that, actually, a lot of work has been done on.

Former General John Allen was a leader of an extensive effort between the U.S. military and the IDF to define the security requirements of a two-state solution and start to come up with solutions—technological, training, joint operations with Jordan, Palestinian forces, Israeli forces, perhaps outside forces as well.

There is a lot of work that has been done on that that is available the next time there are serious negotiations. And I believe solutions can be achieved that will ensure Israel's security and ensure that Palestinians have a sufficient degree of sovereignty that they can absorb it within their own politics.

Mr. DeSANTIS. My time has expired. I yield back.

Ms. ROS-LEHTINEN. Thank you so much, Ron.

And now our ranking member, Mr. Deutch of Florida.

Mr. DEUTCH. Thank you, Madam Chairman.

Ambassador Shapiro, as an Ambassador, you know the importance of every word that comes out of the President of the United States or his representatives in Israel.

So the President acknowledges Jerusalem as the capital of Israel. We have talked about the importance of that statement. The President wasn't willing to commit to Israel's ability to defend itself from potential Iranian bases in Syria. The President backs the end of the martyr payments, then in that same interview said he didn't want to comment on BDS. His Ambassador says settlements are part of Israel. The President then says that settlements are something that complicate and have always complicated making peace.

The President threatened to cut off aid to Palestinians, but the Secretary of State, who is in the region visiting Jordan and Lebanon but not Israel, today says, "I understand President Abbas, his concern about certain steps and decisions taken by the United States."

As someone who was sent to represent the United States by a United States President, how does the Israeli Government and the Israeli public decipher what has seemed to be a whole array of different messages? And in what direction does that lead us, when there are so many messages out there?

Mr. SHAPIRO. Mr. Deutch, I believe the Israeli public and the Israeli Government perceive the Trump administration as very friendly, as very supportive, and I think rightfully so. Obviously, the President's own visit, Vice President Pence's visit, the support Ambassador Haley has provided in the United Nations are ample evidence of that degree of support.

At the same time, what you have just described are a litany of statements that do create a lot of confusion about what indeed is the U.S. policy. People have been, for a year now, trying to decipher what the President means when he talks about the ultimate deal, which, as he describes in other statements that, if you piece together, includes a peace agreement reached between Israelis and Palestinians in direct negotiations that meets Israel's security needs, provides self-determination to Palestinians, and opens Israel's relations to the Arab world. Those are the elements that I think can only be achieved in a two-state solution, and yet he has resisted providing that clarity.

That has led, as you noted earlier, some Israeli leaders to believe that, in fact, he is giving support to move toward annexation or moves that would in other ways make the emergence of an independent Palestinian state later, after there is different and more flexible Palestinian leadership, impossible. And yet there are others who hold on to what he says and say, no, no, he still intends to be the one who will bring about the ultimate deal, as they understand the two-state solution.

More broadly in the region, you mentioned there is confusion and a sense of American withdrawal. I know some people will say that began in the Obama administration. Nevertheless, we are now dealing with a year of the Trump administration.

Secretary Tillerson's trip this week visiting Egypt, Jordan, Lebanon, and Gulf states right after this very dramatic event on Israel's northern border and not coming to Israel has certainly raised questions about what is the U.S. role in supporting Israel's need to defend itself against Iran and Syria.

Mr. DEUTCH. And when—and this is for the panel. Since we don't have someone from the administration to respond to this, I will ask the three of you to speculate.

The question the President was asked, will Israel have to give something in return for the decision on Jerusalem, and his response was, "I think both sides will have to make hard compromises to reach a peace agreement." What do you think he is referring to?

Mr. May?

Mr. MAY. Recognizing Jerusalem as the capital of Israel does not preclude the possibility that a future Palestinian state could have its capital either in eastern Jerusalem or near eastern Jerusalem. I think the President has been clear that that is to be worked out between the two parties.

Mr. DEUTCH. That is the hard compromise?

Mr. al-Omari, what do you think he is referring to?

Mr. MAY. Can I just say I don't think there needs to be a compromise for recognizing Jerusalem as the capital, which it is and which this committee and others has said it is for years and that I know you have.

Mr. DEUTCH. And I have as well. I am just trying to decipher the President. When the President talks about both sides having to make hard compromises, I am just trying to understand what that might mean.

Mr. AL-OMARI. Again, there is no clarity, so we have to basically piece together some of the disparate statements out there.

And it seems to me, on the Israeli side, the difficult compromises they have in mind is, one, you know, two capitals in Jerusalem. And this was lost in the messaging, which was, I think, as was referred to, confused and sometimes contradictory, but, actually, if you look at the fine print, it is there. And I think this is one of the first compromises.

The second is when the President started talking about settlements. He talked about it earlier in his term, and he talked about it this weekend in an interview with an Israeli newspaper in which he said these are not helpful for peace.

These are the kind of compromises that he might be thinking of. But, frankly, we will not know unless there is a plan. And the problem is, in the absence of a plan, others get to fill the void. We have seen messaging coming from Iran, from Qatar, from other countries, that is basically throwing the worst possible light on a future American plan, which has already hardened positions. So there might be some wisdom in withholding a plan, but if we create an expectation and leave a void, others will fill this void in ways that are not good for us.

Mr. DEUTCH. And, Madam Chair, just if I may, Ambassador Shapiro, having served as Ambassador in the Obama administration, where many had expressed concern about the administration laying out a plan and then forcing Israel to accept certain provisions of a plan that most of us believe can only be achieved at the negotiating table, is that exactly what President Trump is contemplating here?

Mr. SHAPIRO. Well, I would be going well beyond my understanding if I told you what President Trump is contemplating.

I do believe that, at some point, greater clarity would actually be helpful. Certainly clarity about the end state of a two-state solution. I believe the clarity about the recognition of Jerusalem as Israel's capital actually was very helpful for all the reasons that have been stated, recognizing a fact and pushing back on a Palestinian myth about the illegitimacy of Jewish history and Jewish presence and sovereignty in Jerusalem.

I think it would have been even better had the other parts of the statement been highlighted to make clear that a Palestinian capital in east Jerusalem as part of the ultimate disposition of this conflict can also be possible.

I think, frankly, the President's—rather, the White House's clarity this week that moves toward annexation of parts of the West Bank would not be helpful and it does not support them was another point of useful clarity.

But, again, we are trying to pull out pieces of this, when, at some point, a presentation of greater clarity on end states and principles, even if we are not moving into immediate negotiations, I do think would be helpful for setting expectations and keeping two states alive for a later negotiation.

Ms. ROS-LEHTINEN. Thank you so much, Ted.

Mr. Zeldin of New York.

Mr. ZELDIN. Well, thank you, Madam Chairman.

I appreciate the conversation here. I have heard "clarity" used a lot as it relates to messaging, policy, and chain of command.

And, Ambassador Shapiro, I am very appreciative of your service to our country. I saw it firsthand in Jerusalem, how well respected you were and the amount of time and energy that you put toward your duties.

I might have a few uncomfortable questions for you, just continuing the conversation of clarity of messaging, policy, and chain of command.

Are you familiar with a meeting that the former Secretary of State had with Hussain Agha in London recently?

Mr. SHAPIRO. I have read press reports about that meeting. That is as much as I know, what everybody else has read in the press.

Mr. ZELDIN. Okay. So you are unable to confirm the accuracy of anything that was allegedly said?

Mr. SHAPIRO. Absolutely unable.

Mr. ZELDIN. Okay. Well, I appreciate that.

And I guess, you know, for the panel, what kind of a message, what kind of impact does it have if all of the reports are true?

What happens if Secretary Kerry had asked Agha to convey to Abbas, "Hold on and be strong," to tell Abbas that he should stay strong in his spirit and play for time, that he will not break, and that he will not yield to President Trump's demands. Reportedly, the former Secretary wanted to convey the message that Trump will not remain in office for a long time. It was reported that Kerry said that within a year there was a good chance that Trump would not be in the White House.

Any reflections from anyone in the panel as far as how that relates to this conversation of clarity on messaging, policy, and chain of command?

Mr. MAY. One hopes that Mr. Kerry's remarks were misreported. If he actually said that, if he actually urged the Palestinians not to negotiate, not to be flexible, not to look for a solution, I think he was very misguided.

Mr. AL-OMARI. Again, I mean, there is—I don't know about the veracity of the reporting, so I can't comment on it.

All I would say is, actually, the Palestinians right now are hearing a different message from some of the U.S. allies in the region.

What they have heard from King Abdullah from Jordan, from President Sisi, and from Mr. Jubeir of Saudi Arabia is the fact that there can be no leader but the United States for the peace process.

The challenge now is how do you create a diplomatic framework in which we can walk them down from that tree and actually resume some sort of negotiation, and there are some interesting ideas out there.

Mr. SHAPIRO. I would just say, again without knowing anything about it other than what has been written in the press, that I do think President Abbas went way, way over the line of acceptable discourse in the speech he gave on January 14th and, really, I believe, signaled the end of his role as a potential participant in negotiations for a two-state solution.

I think this subsequent Palestinian search for an alternative mediator besides the United States is fruitless. I don't believe there is another actor in the international community that can play the role that only the United States has historically played and, I believe, can play in helping even Palestinians achieve their aspirations in a negotiation. It may be that there are roles for others to play, but it is going to be a U.S. leadership role or it is not going to happen.

Mr. ZELDIN. Well, thank you all for that.

And, Ambassador, are you familiar with how it got into the MOU provision that the United States can't provide any more aid than what was agreed upon? Are you familiar with that?

Mr. SHAPIRO. As with previous MOUs, the understanding by both governments was that the levels agreed to in that MOU would be adhered to unless both governments, together, came to the Congress to seek additional funding. That was a provision in previous MOUs, and it was included in the one signed in 2016.

Mr. ZELDIN. So your understanding of that interpretation is that if Congress wants to provide additional aid to Israel nothing in the MOU would prevent it?

Mr. SHAPIRO. Well, my understanding is that Congress is a co-equal branch of government and has the power of the purse and can obviously legislate accordingly in negotiations with the executive branch.

What that MOU committed both governments to was to adhere to those levels of funding unless they mutually agreed that they should be changed. And it was certainly contemplated that in a time of extreme emergency or extreme need that there would be easily the possibility that they could be adjusted, but that the agreement exists so that both sides have predictability of expectation of those levels.

Mr. ZELDIN. A real quick question. Do you believe that the United States should have vetoed U.N. Security Council Resolution 2334?

Mr. SHAPIRO. I am on record saying that was not what I recommended. We do at the time—I believe it would have been—I would have preferred we had ended up with something like the Quartet report of 2016, which was a more balanced document.

Many things have been said about that resolution that I think are not true or very, very highly exaggerated. I don't think it has had anywhere near the effects that people have said. But I am on record saying I had recommended we take another path.

Mr. ZELDIN. Okay.

I really thank you all for being here.

And thank you again, Ambassador, for answering a few tougher questions.

And, again, from my experience firsthand with the Ambassador, seeing him interacting with the Israelis in country, he certainly left a very positive impact on behalf of our country from those efforts and those relationships.

So thank you again for your service.

Mr. SHAPIRO. Thank you, Congressman.

Ms. ROS-LEHTINEN. I echo those remarks. Thank you, Lee.

And Mr. Cicilline of Rhode Island.

Mr. CICILLINE. Thank you, Madam Chair.

And thank you, again, to our witnesses.

I would like to first associate myself with the remarks of my colleague Congresswoman Frankel, that our support of Israel has always been a bipartisan approach; it is very longstanding in this committee and this Congress and this country. I think it is because of the shared values between our two countries. And it makes the absence of a coherent policy in this area particularly alarming to many of us.

I would like to report that Secretary Tillerson, at a press conference just moments ago in Jordan, said that he has seen elements of President Trump's plan for peace in the Middle East and that the proposal is fairly well-advanced. And he wasn't able to give a timeline but says it has been under development for several months. So who knows? There may actually be a plan, which hopefully we will learn about someday.

But I hear from the really thoughtful testimony of the three witnesses that there is a recognition that this is not a moment—Ambassador, you said that there is no chance for breakthrough or even resumption of negotiations.

Do the other two witnesses agree? Yes.

So, while there is a lot of talk about the big deal that is secretly being planned, it seems like the people who actually know the most about this conflict in this region think that we have to be much more pragmatic and find some small steps in the right direction, as the Ambassador said, that will preserve the viability of a two state, two people living side-by-side in peace and prosperity.

And I am wondering, what are those steps? What can we do, what can the United States do, to promote the viability and try to preserve that?

And I know a lot of the testimony, your written testimony, talks about succession planning and, kind of, the leadership that is required. And, in fact, Mr. May, in your written testimony, you said, "The administration, with congressional support, should attempt to work with Saudi Arabia, the UAE, and other Sunni Arab partners, as well as any pragmatic elements within the Palestinian Authority to create a leadership succession plan, one that will empower Palestinian leaders who are open to conflict resolution and do not see peaceful coexistence with Israel as tantamount to defeat. Without such a plan in place, the possibility of chaos, violence, and instability following Mr. Abbas' passing looms large."

So I just wonder what the panel's thoughts are. I think everyone agrees that leadership in the Palestinian Authority is necessary. It seems unlikely, in this moment, that there will be leadership that will actually be serious about the peace process. But what is your assessment of that? And what is the likelihood that some of the changes in the region, particularly with Saudi Arabia and potential new partnerships or cooperation with Israel, provide some leverage? Is there anything that we can do to promote that?

Maybe start with you, Ambassador, and then just go down the line. I know there are a lot of questions there.

Mr. SHAPIRO. Sure.

I do believe that the now open secret of the strategic cooperation that exists between Saudi Arabia, the United Arab Emirates, other Gulf states, other moderate Sunni states, and Israel is a real opportunity. It is an opportunity for those states to demonstrate to the Israeli public, to the Palestinian public, to their own publics that this is not something to be kept hidden and to actually demonstrate what the future can look like of a region in which there are open borders and open trade and exchanges of all kinds. That should be able to be done now, regardless of what is happening on the Israeli-Palestinian arena directly.

I believe they also can be partners in helping, let's say, put Palestinian expectations in a reasonable frame of mind, that it will have to include recognition of Israel as a Jewish state, that it will have to end the myth of a mass return of refugees to the state of Israel, pre-1948 Israel.

So there are things that they can do, and those don't need to wait for the resumption of negotiations.

Mr. CICILLINE. Okay.

Mr. May?

Mr. MAY. Yes. Look, I think that we have a leadership crisis now. I think we all agree on this panel, and I think you do as well in the subcommittee, that the Israelis cannot make peace with Hamas, that is not realistic. And that Mahmoud Abbas has taken himself out of the running as a partner for peace. So we have a leadership crisis now. We have a succession crisis on the horizon. I think it is important to begin to address that now. What hap- pens when Mahmoud Abbas, who is 82, not in great health, a heavy smoker, what happens when he passes from the scene? As I say in my testimony, under Palestinian basic law, initially some- body from Hamas takes over.

And then the idea of free elections—we haven't had free elections. We haven't had, I think, free elections ever. The last elections were a long time ago. As we said, Mahmoud Abbas is in the 13th year of a 4-year term.

I think honesty is important. I agree with the Ambassador. In the beginning, not at the end, of the negotiation process, certain things should be established: One, that "two states" means a Jewish state and a Palestinian state. That absolutely is important.

I think it is important, too, that UNRWA provide transparency. We do not have 5 million refugees who must be settled in Israel, the Israelis will never accept it. We have probably 20,000 or 30,000. There is a report that makes this clear. That report should be unclassified so Congress gets to see it.

Mr. CICILLINE. Mr. al-Omari?

Mr. AL-OMARI. If I may, the issue of succession and the issue of the Arab states, but I would start, maybe, with a disagreement with my colleague. I think President Abbas can be a partner for peace, but he has to retract and walk back the unacceptable statements that he made. But, ultimately, we have to make peace between Israelis and Palestinians with the current—or with the leaders that they have.

Now, that said, when it comes to succession, the first thing about it is what not to do. We cannot pick a successor for the Palestinians. We have never been good in managing other people's politics, and I don't think we should do this right now.

Instead, we should take our cue from President George W. Bush when he pushed for reform in the Palestinian Authority. And he pushed very hard, and he created an international coalition, European and Arab. That was key in creating a political space. That political space allowed new leaders to emerge, including Salam Fayyad and people like Salam Fayyad. We have to do the same. We have to prioritize reform, both governance and political, and let the Palestinian system produce its own. And there are plenty of talented people right there.

In terms of the Arabs, I do believe that expecting open Arab-Israeli relations right now is unrealistic. Desirable as it may be, it is unrealistic, for a simple reason: The Arabs are getting what they need from this relationship under the table. Why should they pay the price to go over the table?

Instead, we should test the Arabs' resolve in terms of how they approach the Palestinians, and that is two things. First of all, they have to be a key actor in managing the issue of succession. They tried that a couple of years ago but walked back because they felt there was no American cover. We should give them that cover. And, two, to actually get them in private, not in public, because they won't do it in public, in private to engage in conversations with Abbas to lower the expectations. And when I say "conversations," that, of course, includes pressure. We can bring them in—again, don't have an objective that is too high, they will not come in. Have a realistic one, test them on that, and lock them in the process.

Mr. CICILLINE. Thank you so much.

I yield back, Madam Chairman.

Ms. ROS-LEHTINEN. Thank you so much, David.

Ambassador Wagner.

Mrs. WAGNER. Thank you, Madam Chairwoman.

I am a proud supporter of the democratic state of Israel. Israel is a beacon of peace and human rights in the Middle East. And though I am increasingly pessimistic that peace negotiations are going to progress in the near term, I am adamant that we continue building the bilateral relationship and also rejuvenate our efforts to promote Palestinian reform.

Mr. May and Ambassador Shapiro, very quickly, you both mentioned in your testimonies that Israel and Palestine have thriving high-tech sectors. Do you think this is an area where both sides can cooperate?

Mr. MAY. Well, in theory, I do, and I think it is very necessary. I think a viable Palestinian state, a Palestinian state that would not be a permanent ward of the international donor community, must have economic cooperation with Israel, and that would include the high-tech sector.

But, in order to do that, you have to have a Palestinian leadership that favors economic normalization and other forms of normalization. You can't have BDS.

Right now, what you are describing, which is very necessary, as necessary for Palestinians, who should have jobs and prosperity, as it is for Israel. But right now we do not have a Palestinian leadership that favors that or encourages that. We should press for that.

Mrs. WAGNER. Mr. Shapiro?

Mr. SHAPIRO. Congresswoman, there is already engagement between the emerging Palestinian high-tech sector, where there is a lot of talent, and the very, very vibrant Israeli high-tech sector. In fact, I think one finds that the Palestinians who engage in those professions are among the least politicized and among the most pragmatic and the most forward-leaning in terms of engagement with Israeli colleagues that there are.

There are some good examples, Israeli companies that have set up R&D centers in Palestinian towns, such as the new city of Rawabi.

In my written testimony, I highlighted an article in Foreign Affairs magazine from last summer which lays out an approach the United States could take to support the emergence of that Palestinian high-tech sector, completely bypassing the Palestinian Authority and, in fact, I think, empowering the most—the elements of Palestinian society that are most forward-leaning and the ones we want to work with.

Mrs. WAGNER. I have a lot of questions and a short amount of time.

Mr. al-Omari, you spoke about prospects for engagement with moderate Arab states. Regional powers like Saudi Arabia, Jordan,

Egypt, and the UAE have much to gain from a coalition with the U.S. and Israel on security coordination against Iran.

But when Iran sent a drone into Israeli airspace on Saturday, prompting counter-strikes against Iranian-built targets in Syria, in which Israel lost an F-16 fighter, only—only—the United States of America expressed support for Israel.

Is this representative of the way Arab states will try to navigate the Israeli-Iranian rivalry, sir?

Mr. AL-OMARI. These Arab states have their own public opinion to take into account, so when it comes to official messaging, most of them were silent. But what is very interesting this time, is if you look at the state media, or the state-controlled media in these Arab countries, if you look, for example, at Qatari-controlled media, it celebrated the downing of the F16. It celebrated it. If you look at the Saudi-owned media, which is active in the UAE and Egypt, in particular, there was almost no mention highlighting the Iranian intrusion into Israeli sovereignty. So you are not going to see it now in terms of official opening. They still have to be very careful about the public, but we are seeing a very different tone when it comes to public messaging. That is important. That needs to be encouraged, I believe.

Mrs. WAGNER. Thank you. Ambassador Shapiro, and I want to thank you for your service, too, also, sir. I appreciated that you highlighted the reprehensible remarks Abbas made in January regarding the Jewish people's historic connection to Israel. That behavior is wildly inappropriate in a leader charged with participating in serious peace talks. You have a deep familiarity with actors on both sides of the conflict.

Looking beyond Abbas, as we have talked a little bit, and Mr. May has mentioned this, too, is there a new generation of thoughtful and proactive Palestinian leaders who are willing to work with the United States and Israel?

Mr. SHAPIRO. There is certainly an emerging generation, but I have to say, one of the great flaws of the current generation of Palestinian leaders is their failure to really empower a next generation.

People often ask me what is the succession for Abbas, and I say: It is the biggest black box in the Middle East. I don't know any Palestinian who really knows. I don't know any Israeli who really knows. I don't know any other Arab in other countries who really knows either. We can all name eight or 10 people who might have a role. I agree strongly that we will not be able to pick a successor to Abbas, and if we try, we will probably screw it up.

There are actors in the region who might be able to help steer that succession in the first instance toward some of the more moderate possibilities, and in the second instance, try to help build up that more moderate, business-minded, pragmatic Palestinian generation, which has, so far, really been excluded from politics.

Mrs. WAGNER. Thank you. I appreciate that. My time is expired. I yield back, Madam Chair.

Ms. ROS-LEHTINEN. Thank you so much, Ambassador.

And now, Mr. Schneider of Illinois.

Mr. SCHNEIDER. Thank you, Madam Chairman, and thanks again to the witnesses.

As I said before, not a day goes by that I don't pray for peace for Israel. To my core, I believe peace is only going to be realized by a two-state solution, the Jewish democratic state of Israel living in peace and security side-by-side, an Arab state.

Unfortunately, I personally don't believe such a peace is on the near horizon. Now we heard earlier, one of my colleagues said something different, so I have a number of questions.

Do any of the three of you believe that we are closer to peace today than at any other time in the last 70 years?

Mr. SHAPIRO. I do not.

Mr. AL-OMARI. It is almost ironic in the sense that politically, we certainly are not. The content of what peace looks like has never been clearer than it has been in the past. This is different from the 1990s and the early 2000s, where we had to guess what peace looks like. We know what it looks like. What we don't have are the leaders who will get us there.

Mr. MAY. But I would also say that we have never been close to peace. We have never been close to peace for coexistence or to a resolution of the conflict. We need to learn from the mistakes of past peace processes if we are going to get anywhere this time around.

Mr. SCHNEIDER. Fair enough. I am thinking how to best put that in words. I am going to put it in my own words.

Do you believe that the Israeli people want peace?

Mr. MAY. Profoundly.

Mr. SHAPIRO. Absolutely.

Mr. AL-OMARI. I would say it is actually opinion polls, for what it is worth, show an erosion of support for peace. An erosion based on the belief that peace is not attainable. If you ask Israelis, and, by the way, Palestinians, they will tell you: We want peace. We don't think the other side wants it. Therefore, it is not going to happen. So we are starting to see an abandonment out of despair, not out of rejection of the idea.

Mr. SCHNEIDER. So I will draw a distinction between confidence that peace is on the horizon, Bashana Haba'ah, and the difference between wanting peace. Having lived in Israel 30 years ago, having been to Israel countless times, all the Israelis I know want peace, want peace for their children, want peace for their neighbors.

Who, if anyone, is positioned to be Israel's partner for peace at this moment, within the Palestinians?

Mr. AL-OMARI. In theory, you see the position of the PA continue to support the two-state solution. In practice, we have seen many policies and statements that makes it very difficult. What I would say is, again, we saw this during the Bush presidency where if we push for the kind of reform that allows voices—and these voices exists—to come out, whether on reform or in terms of promoting pragmatic peace-loving policies, they will emerge.

However, if we allow the current trend of despotism, of totalitarianism, to continue in the PA, these voices are scared. These voices feel that they are persecuted and, therefore, they will not emerge. A lot depends on our ability to create and help create this political space for these voices to emerge. And as the Ambassador said, the political mechanism for them to be empowered and to actually be well-positioned to become effective political actors.

Mr. SCHNEIDER. Okay. Mr. May.

Mr. MAY. I don't disagree with my colleague. I would just say this: There are no voices in the Palestinian Authority who say, not only do we want our own state, they do, but we want that state to no longer be in conflict with the state of Israel. Gaza was—as you know, in 2005 the Israeli left Gaza, it did not become Singapore in the Mediterranean; it became a basis for terrorism, missiles and terror tunnels against Israel. The West Bank could do that, too.

Mr. SCHNEIDER. And thousands of rockets over the years. I am going to shift gears a little bit.

With Iran establishing a permanent presence in Syria, Iran building indigenous rocket missile capability in Syria and in Lebanon, and the humanitarian crisis brewing in Gaza, Hamas. Abbas' message delivered a few weeks ago, and as was said, earlier Abbas, in the 13th year of his 4-year term, increasing terrorism activity in Sinai.

I was going to ask a question, but I will make a statement. I think it is fair to say that Israel faces more threats now on its borders than it has in a while, and it is of grave concern. This is highlighted, obviously, in the incursion this past weekend of an Iranian drone into Israeli territory, and an F16 shot down over Israeli territory.

My question is, and I am going to start with you, Ambassador Shapiro, what signal does it send to Israel and the region that while Secretary of State Tillerson is in the region, he hasn't found it convenient to stand shoulder to shoulder with the Israelis and send a message to the world that we will protect, we will work with Israel, we will help Israel defend herself?

Mr. SHAPIRO. It is a missed opportunity. Not because it means the administration does not support Israel's right to defend itself. It stated that clearly. But the demonstration of that commitment in real time, during crises, that the security coordination—where the strategic level, the tactical level, and the diplomatic level is taking place is always beneficial. Frankly, I think it would have even been more beneficial for Secretary Tillerson, for his credibility on his other stops in the region, to show that he stood shoulder to shoulder with our closest ally.

When he showed up in Cairo and Amman and the Gulf, and now in Beirut, and cannot report directly to them on the conversations he has had, and the ability to say where we are backing certain Israeli security requirements and red lines, I think it makes him less credible and, therefore, it harms the United States.

Mr. SCHNEIDER. Mr. al-Omari.

Mr. AL-OMARI. In terms of actual support for Israel, I think this administration is clearly supporting Israel.

Mr. SCHNEIDER. Absolutely.

Mr. AL-OMARI. Yet in terms of the messaging, I believe, and I agree with the Ambassador, this is a missed opportunity. In general, this administration has not yet managed to fine-tune its messaging to the region. This was an important message to be sent. They missed it. However, we have a bigger problem. If you zoom out a little bit, many of the strategic situations that you described are a result of a vacuum in the region. And the vacuum that we have not filled yet. We hear a lot of great pronouncements, but as of yet, these have not been translated into a policy. And until we see a policy and a strategy, I fear that not only for Israel, but also for other U.S. allies in the region, the strategic outlook will remain quite grim.

Mr. SCHNEIDER. Mr. May.

Mr. MAY. I will just say that I agree with my colleagues on this point.

Mr. SCHNEIDER. Thank you. And just for the record, with my colleague, let me first associate with what my colleague Ms. Frankel said, the support for Israel has always been bipartisan. It is critical that it always remains bipartisan. The loss of that would be a terrible loss for the U.S.-Israel relationship and security of both our nations.

My colleague, Mr. Mast, and I sent a letter to Secretary of State Tillerson asking him to stop in Israel to make a clear statement.

As was said, the U.S. stands with Israel. That remains as true today as it was before. At this moment, the more we can demonstrate it, I think the better it will be. And with that, I yield back.

Ms. ROS-LEHTINEN. Thank you, Brad. Mr. Rohrabacher of California.

Mr. ROHRABACHER. Let me just say I think the administration is doing well in projecting those policies that will bring peace rather than the 8 years we have had that have brought chaos and a rise of power of radical Islam, the undermining of moderate forces in the Middle East, and the elimination of secular governments. That is what the last administration, which was so definable and so coherent, gave this administration.

And let me just say, I think the policy is really good. That is, we are going to do things. Specific things, the policies will be recognized as supporting Israel, as long as the Palestinians are unwilling to do those things that will bring peace. For example, suggesting that we are not going to give aid to the Palestinians if they continue to attack Israel, and we are not going to give aid to those countries that are participating in that.

For example, we are recognizing Jerusalem for the first time as the capital of Israel. Those are tangible. Those aren't incoherent. And those send a signal. They send a signal to those people who would rely on bloodshed and terrorism to achieve their goal. Those people will get that message as we continue with specific policies that makes sense to achieving peace in that region, by eliminating those people who believe in violence and terrorism from their position of leverage.

I used to believe in the two-state solution. I was a backer of a two-state solution. I thought, there you go. I don't dislike the Palestinian people, I think they are wonderful. I think most people in this world are good people. But there is a conflict here that we have to face as adults, and unless we do, we are not going to bring peace any closer, either for the Palestinians or the Israelis.

But as I mentioned earlier, Israel gave up authority on large parts of the West Bank, totally in Gaza, withdrew from the Sinai, did so many of these things, and only two demands: Don't use violence and terrorism against us, and, please, recognize our right to exist. Well, the Palestinians have done neither of those. So what have they given up? Nothing. And we are suppose to put pressure on Israel and blame them when they have given up nothing and Israel has given up all of this?

Yeah, all we need from the Palestinians is a recognition that they don't have a right of return. By claiming the right of return—please correct me, and I am putting this out to the panel—isn't the right of return basically someone who says that we don't believe Israel has a right to exist? Isn't that what it really says, if someone refuses to say: No, we don't have a right to send in millions of Palestinians into what is now Israel?

And number two, of course, we should expect, the Palestinians to say and do, we are not going to sponsor terrorist attacks from those territories that Israel gave up authority on, whether the Gaza Strip or the West Bank.

Yes.

Mr. MAY. Mr. Congressman, I think this gets back to my point about UNRWA. The U.N. High Commissioner for refugees recognizes refugees as people who fled from a land. UNRWA has a different definition; the son, the grandson, the great grandson, the great, great grandson can be a refugee. So you have gone from about 700,000 refugees—about the same number as Jews who fled and were made refugees from Arab and Muslim lands in the same period, late 1940s-early 1950s—to today, about 15 million so-called refugees, who are not refugees under the normal definition.

You would have 14 million in just a few years based on current demographics. At that point, the population of Israel now is only 8 million. About 20 to 25 percent are minorities now. So what you are saying, if you are saying these refugees—so-called—more than 5 million of them, have to be settled in Israel, you are saying that Israel will become a Palestinian majority state, Hamas will remain as an entity, and Jordan would be what it is, a Palestinian majority state in eastern Palestine.

Yes, this is why we need honesty. If we know that there are 20,000 or 30,000 people who left in 1948, we can figure out something to do with them. Five million people, that is a way to say Israel cannot exist as a Jewish state.

Mr. ROHRABACHER. Can we have a two-state solution as long as one side says, we have a right to send in millions of people into your country?

Mr. AL-OMARI. First of all, when it comes to a right of return, I think it was very clear from the early stages of negotiations. We saw it in Camp David, and ever since that, the Palestinians would not ask for implementation of a right of return. We saw this clearly in the Arab Peace Initiative, which was produced in Beirut——

Mr. ROHRABACHER. So you are saying the Palestinians' position is not that they are not demanding a right of return?

Mr. AL-OMARI. What I am saying is that in negotiations and in the Arab Peace Initiative, it was made very clear that any return would be subject to agreement with Israel——

Mr. ROHRABACHER. I talked to a lot of Palestinians—and as I say, I am open-minded to their arguments, they are human beings, and should be treated that way—and none of them will agree that they don't have a right of return.

Mr. AL-OMARI. Except this is, again, is the official position. But, if I may, on the one issue of security—I mean—this is something that I have heard in some interventions. Palestinian Israeli Security Cooperation is, at its best, since the 1990s, and by the recognition of military and security establishment. We heard, actually, the Israeli chief of staff only 2 weeks ago talk about it. This weekend, two Israelis strayed into a Palestinian city, Jenin, and Palestinian security forces actually extracted them.

We see a lot of security support. There is one thing to be said for Abbas, he is against violence, and he has been persistently against violence. When it comes to security, I think the track record is good. And by the way, great, great credit goes to the U.S. through the Office of the Security Coordinator which did this, and to Jordan which was shepherding this point.

Mr. ROHRABACHER. We can talk at length, but when you condense it down to, do you believe that millions of people should be able to go into Israel, and they refuse to say, no, we are not demanding that, well that is the stumbling block. And I would hope that we, as I say, I had faith in the two-state solution, but I am not stupid. And certainly, the Israelis, after suffering casualties from this situation, aren't stupid. If people believe in peace there, they should say, we don't believe in the right of return for millions of people, and we are going to cease killing a bunch of Israelis with rockets and terrorists attacks. That is all. That would bring peace. But we don't see it.

And so that is why this administration is not pressuring Israel, but instead, is doing some things to show we are willing to back up Israel because they are open to these solutions, but we don't have any fear about cutting the Palestinians off if they are not going to go in that direction.

Mr. SHAPIRO. Congressman, if I may.

Mr. ROHRABACHER. Yes, sir.

Mr. SHAPIRO. When Prime Minister Netanyahu in his Bar-Ilan University speech in 2009, spoke about a two-state solution for the first time, a demilitarized Palestinian state that recognize the Jewish state, he was essentially hitting on the two issues you have raised: Ceasing to call into question Israel's status as a Jewish state, including through the perpetuation of the myth of the return of many millions of Palestinian refugees and their descendants; and the demilitarization as the one-word description of a security regime in which Israel can be guaranteed that what happened in Gaza after they left is not repeated in the West Bank, which would be a completely unacceptable outcome.

Every negotiation that the United States has been involved in, including the ones I participated in, recognized those requirements and tried to steer toward those outcomes. And I absolutely agree with you, those are essential components of a two-state solution. And it may be, for the reasons we have been discussing, that at this point, there is no Palestinian leadership, and it may be that there is no Israeli coalition at the moment that is really committed to the same outcomes.

My only concern as a matter of U.S. interest, is if, while waiting for that Palestinian leadership to emerge and that Palestinian change of attitude to emerge, the two-state solution sort of falls off the cliff to where once they are there, it is impossible to achieve it, that, too, will call into question Israel's status as a Jewish and democratic state. That, too, will pose long-term security risk to Israel. And that, too, will pose a real harm to U.S. interest.

Ms. ROS-LEHTINEN. Thank you so much.

Mr. ROHRABACHER. Don't hold your breath while you are waiting for it.

Ms. ROS-LEHTINEN. Thank you so much, Dana.

And Ms. Frankel of Florida. Thank you, Lois.

Ms. FRANKEL. Thank you, Madam Chair. I wanted to start off where I ended my earlier remarks, which were how important I think it is that we look at this issue of the peace and security of Israel, and maintaining Israel as a democratic Jewish state in a bipartisan way.

That does not mean that we are not allowed to question the policies and the actions of different administrations. I think, though, that intent and motive, I don't question the intent and motive of this administration, nor our past administration in terms of wanting to accomplish this goal. And in that regard, I just—I want to thank our chairwoman, and also our ranking member, who has left the meeting because of a very serious emergency in his district, but they are an example to me of just phenomenal leadership in trying to get a grasp on these issues. And I want to thank you, Madam Chair. I really do. And I thank Representative Deutch.

We heard, and I don't know, maybe Madam Chair, you would remember this, but we heard the testimony within the last few years of Robert Wexler, who, I believe, works for the Abraham Center for Peace. I want to try to paraphrase what I remember him saying, and then I would like to have your comment.

"The Jewish population from the Mediterranean Sea to the Jordan River will soon be a minority." I would, as I said before, I believe it is a bipartisan desire here to see Israel with secure borders that endures a democratic and Jewish state. The demographic trends are not working in Israel's favor. And it just seems to me that time is on the side of the Palestinians. I would just like you to comment on that observation.

Mr. SHAPIRO. Congresswoman, I think those demographic figures are well known and fairly well understood. And I, indeed, think it very much underscores why Prime Minister Netanyahu, after many years in which he did not support that outcome, did support a two-state solution. And more specifically, said what he wants to avoid is a binational state. And that is what you are, I think, referring to. A situation which under the framework of one state, you have basically equivalent Jewish and Arab populations. And then Israel faces some very, very profound choices about whether to focus on maintaining the Jewish character or the democratic character, and it is very difficult, maybe impossible, to do both.

And so for all the reasons we have been stating, including much responsibility that falls on the Palestinian side, or at least on the Palestinian leadership side, we aren't close to solving that. But if we reach a stage where that becomes impossible, then those really terrible choices that face Israel and face us as Israel's closest ally and where our interest is bound up in those choices come into play.

Mr. AL-OMARI. The one-state outcome, and I don't call it a solution because it is not a solution. A one-state outcome is in no one's interest. And in that regard, time is not on anyone's side. This one-state construct means the end of Zionism, which is really about the right of the Jewish people to their own state. You would have a binational state, no longer a Jewish state, but it is also the end of Palestinian nationalism. The desire of the Palestinians to have their own state and their own representation.

Time will kill both ideas. And in the meantime, more and more people will die, more and more people will suffer. That is why I am still a believer that the two-state solution is the only option. The question now is how do we do it? In a smart way, in a way that will get the objective and actually get us there in a measured way that understands the political constraints of the reality today.

Mr. MAY. I think, Congresswoman, that there is some debate over the demographics, but I think we can put that aside. The pivotal question seems to me, when you say that time is on the Palestinian side, what does that mean?

Does that mean Israel needs to make concessions that would sacrifice and compromise its security? I don't think so, I think the Israelis are open to a two-state solution. I think we have seen that. But it has to be, again, two states for two peoples with the Palestinians recognizing that one of those peoples is the Jewish people. We don't have that at this moment.

Failing that, there will not be movement. And I don't think one can assume that, therefore, they will be moving to a one-state outcome because a one-state outcome would mean that the Israelis are making citizens of millions of people who believe that they will be martyrs if they plunge a knife into the throat of a Jew. I do not see Israelis doing that, now or ever. I think they are resolute that they are going to protect what they built, which is a Jewish state in part of their ancient homeland.

Ms. FRANKEL. Thank you.

Ms. ROS-LEHTINEN. Thank you so much, Lois.

I just had a question about U.N. action. What we think will happen or not happen. And as we know, Abu Mazen has always approached his goal of realizing a Palestinian state on a dual track, direct negotiations, supposedly, with Israel, and then unilateral statehood schemes at the U.N. And I would argue that he only feigns interest in the former in order to place greater emphasis in the latter.

So he will be at the U.N. Security Council next week, likely pushing for U.N. action. We can't predict what will happen, but we can expect that he will push resolutions at UNESCO, and mirroring his speech that we have all talked about where he claims that Jews have no historical or cultural ties to Jerusalem.

So given his efforts on unilateral statehood, should we even try to engage him at this point, bring him to the table? And what do you think will happen, if anything, at the U.N. in this coming session?

And we will start with you, Mr. al-Omari.

Mr. AL-OMARI. In the U.N., I suspect he will do what he has been doing so far, which is actually playing a balancing act. On the one hand, he wants to create noise back home. This is a political tool for raising his political popularity back home. We will hear a tough speech, though I hope that he will not, again, cross these lines. But what he will not do is join any U.N. agency which triggers American cuts of support for the agency.

After UNESCO, he got under a lot of pressure from many to say not do that again. So he will join treaties, et cetera. I suspect he will also ask to join the U.N. in order to get a U.S. veto, because a U.S. veto looks good for him. He sounds tough to his population. He will do that. There is no doubt.

What we need to do is a two-track strategy. On the one hand, we need to make it very clear that there is a red line that he cannot cross, and I think we need to deliver this through our allies, not only directly. But also, start constructing a ladder to get him down from that tree. And that ladder is a quartet with the addition possibly of Jordan and Egypt with American leadership. I think if we create that, I think we can start bringing him down from that, and we can resume normal diplomacy.

Ms. ROS-LEHTINEN. Thank you. Anyone else? Thank you, Cliff.

Mr. MAY. Let me just say, Madam Chairman, the U.N. has not and I think we can expect, will not play a positive role in terms of trying to resolve the Palestinian-Israeli conflict. And the U.N. Human Rights Council is probably the worst agency within the U.N.

It is a collection of chronic and egregious violators of human rights that bashes Israel constantly. This is something else I would urge the Congress to look at and see what can be done about it. U.N. reform, reform of this agency and of UNRWA, I think is imperative, and I have recommendations along those lines in my testimony.

Ms. ROS-LEHTINEN. Good. Thank you so much. Mr. Ambassador.

Mr. SHAPIRO. I think as was stated, President Abbas will probably try to play some of the same cards he has played before. And I think the U.S. position needs to remain that something that recognizes that a Palestinian state that has not emerged through negotiations is not something that we can support. I think that will continue to be the U.S. position.

I actually think, though, where he may find a more fertile ground to make some progress, in his mind, is by going to European governments and trying to promote recognition of a Palestinian state there. Of course, many other countries around the world already recognize a Palestinian state. We do not. And that has not been brought about by negotiations. But the European governments are sort of the prize for him. It may be that that is where he will seek to try to counterpressure what he feels he is getting from the United States, and I think there are some governments that are considering that. That is obviously going to be an important diplomatic challenge for the administration to focus on.

Ms. ROS-LEHTINEN. Thank you so much, Mr. Ambassador. And thank you to our excellent row of panelists, thank you to the audience, and all the members who visited today.

So with that, the subcommittee is adjourned. Thank you to all.

[Whereupon, at 4:05 p.m., the subcommittee was adjourned.]

APPENDIX

MATERIAL SUBMITTED FOR THE RECORD

SUBCOMMITTEE HEARING NOTICE
COMMITTEE ON FOREIGN AFFAIRS
U.S. HOUSE OF REPRESENTATIVES
WASHINGTON, DC 20515-6128

Subcommittee on the Middle East and North Africa
Ileana Ros-Lehtinen (R-FL), Chairman

February 7, 2018

TO: MEMBERS OF THE COMMITTEE ON FOREIGN AFFAIRS

You are respectfully requested to attend an OPEN hearing of the Committee on Foreign Affairs to be held by the Subcommittee on the Middle East and North Africa in Room 2172 of the Rayburn House Office Building (and available live on the Committee website at http://www.ForeignAffairs.house.gov).

DATE: Wednesday, February 14, 2018

TIME: 2:00 p.m.

SUBJECT: Israel, the Palestinians, and the Administration's Peace Plan

WITNESSES: Mr. Clifford M. May
                  Founder and President
                  Foundation for Defense of Democracies

                  Mr. Ghaith al-Omari
                  Senior Fellow
                  Irwin Levy Family Program on the U.S.-Israel Strategic Relationship
                  The Washington Institute for Near East Policy

                  The Honorable Daniel B. Shapiro
                  Distinguished Visiting Fellow
                  Institute for National Security Studies, Tel Aviv
                  (Former United States Ambassador to Israel)

By Direction of the Chairman

COMMITTEE ON FOREIGN AFFAIRS

MINUTES OF SUBCOMMITTEE ON _______ *Middle East and North Africa* _______ HEARING

Day __*Wednesday*__ Date ____*02.14.18*____ Room ____*2172*____

Starting Time __*2:25 p.m.*__ Ending Time __*4:05 p.m.*__

Recesses |____| (____to ____) (____to ____) (____to ____) (____to ____) (____to ____) (____to ____)

Presiding Member(s)

Chairman Ros-Lehtinen

Check all of the following that apply:

Open Session ☑   Electronicall   y Recorded (taped) ☑
Executive (closed) Session ☐   Stenographic Record ☑
Televised ☑

TITLE OF HEARING:

Israel, the Palestinians and the Administration's Peace Plan

SUBCOMMITTEE MEMBERS PRESENT:

GOP- Chair Ros-Lehtinen, Reps. Chabot, DeSantis, Zeldin, Donovan, Wagner, Mast, Fitzpatrick, Curtis
Dem- RK Deutch, Reps. Connolly, Cicilline, Frankel, Schneider, Suozzi, Lieu

NON-SUBCOMMITTEE MEMBERS PRESENT: *(Mark with an * if they are not members of full committee.)*

HEARING WITNESSES: Same as meeting notice attached? Yes ☑ No ☐
(If "no", please list below and include title, agency, department, or organization.)

STATEMENTS FOR THE RECORD: *(List any statements submitted for the record.)*

Rep. Connolly's Statement for the Record

TIME SCHEDULED TO RECONVENE _______
or
TIME ADJOURNED __*4:05 p.m.*__

Subcommittee Staff Associate

Statement for the Record
Submitted by Mr. Connolly of Virginia

Support for a two-state solution to the Israeli-Palestinian conflict has been longstanding, bipartisan U.S. policy in the Middle East. During his first year in office, Trump has issued statements and taken steps that erode widespread, bipartisan support for a two-state solution. The Trump Administration's actions have pushed the Israelis and Palestinians further away from peace, undermined U.S. credibility as a mediator of this conflict, and threatened U.S. national security interests in a critical and unstable part of the world.

Trump designated his son-in-law, Jared Kushner, as his personal envoy for Middle East peace. But Kushner's efforts have been dogged by a steep learning curve for a man with zero experience in high-stakes diplomatic negotiations. Authorities have an ongoing investigation into credible allegations against Kushner involving national security issues, and yet the White House has refused to explain its decision not to suspend his security clearance, per protocol, despite a request from all Democratic members of the House Oversight and Government Reform Committee.

The Trump Administration has repeatedly refused to reaffirm the U.S. commitment to a two-state solution, including at a press conference with Israeli Prime Minister Benjamin Netanyahu last February. In response, I led a letter with Rep. David Price and 189 other members of Congress urging Trump to clarify the United States' continued support for a negotiated settlement that leads to a sustainable two-state solution to the Israeli-Palestinian conflict. There can be no substitute for direct, bilateral negotiations between the two parties to achieve a sustainable two-state solution. And let's be clear, a two-state solution is the only option that would allow Israel to maintain its identity as a Jewish and democratic state.

In December, Trump announced that the United States would recognize Jerusalem as Israel's capital and begin the process of moving our embassy from Tel Aviv. When President Jimmy Carter sat down at the negotiating table with Egyptian President Anwar Sadat and Israeli Prime Minister Menachem Begin at Camp David in 1978, he reiterated that Jerusalem's final status would not be decided unilaterally. Every successive U.S. administration since then has upheld that approach. President Trump's declaration abandoned that commitment, sparked a wave of protests and unrest throughout the region, and brought his own Administration's efforts to achieve peace to a standstill. There has been zero engagement between the Trump Administration and Palestinian officials since the Jerusalem announcement.

This week, the Trump Administration's FY 2019 budget proposed to cut U.S. assistance to the West Bank and Gaza by 14 percent. Last month, the State Department notified the U.N. Relief and Works Agency, which provides humanitarian assistance to Palestinian refugees in the West Bank and Gaza, that the U.S. was reducing its contribution by 83 percent. Reducing aid for the Palestinians, especially at a time when prospects for peace are so dim, is a recipe for disaster that is likely to further destabilize the region. By providing aid, the United States and its allies are laying the groundwork in the hopes that a future, long-lasting peace is viable. Cutting off aid suddenly could have severe consequences for responsible governance, humanitarian needs, and the future of Middle East peace. That is why, when the full Committee considered H.R. 1164, the Taylor Force Act, I was glad to successfully offer an amendment that would protect funding to the Palestinian Authority for programs that provide vaccinations to children.

The United States and Israel have a special bond rooted in shared values and national security interests. The continuation of this relationship and the prospect of a sustainable end to the conflict require firm, yet balanced, leadership from the United States. The U.S. has pursued peace negotiations, blocked one-sided United Nations Security Council Resolutions, condemned Israeli settlements in the West Bank, conditioned aid to the Palestinian Authority in order to combat violence, and helped build institutions within Palestinian society that facilitate progress towards a negotiated, two-state solution. We must do everything in our power to foster peace and prosperity for our greatest friend and ally in the Middle East.

Maintenance of the status quo is one of the greatest threats facing Israel today. Rather than positioning the United States as a supporter and honest broker of a lasting peace, the Trump Administration has charged a diplomatic neophyte with striking "the ultimate deal," and undermined the prospects for peace between Israel and the Palestinians at every turn. Besieged on all sides and locked in conflict in perpetuity is not a future we should accept for the United States' closest ally in the Middle East.

www.ingramcontent.com/pod-product-compliance
Lightning Source LLC
Chambersburg PA
CBHW080034260726
48658CB00007B/2611